Human Rights Education and Peacebuilding

This book assesses the role of human rights education (HRE) in the peacebuilding field.

Today, most governments, international organizations and non-governmental organizations recognize the importance of human rights in peace- and democracy-building activities in post-conflict regions. However, compared with other components of peacebuilding, little attention and funding has been given to the cultivation of human rights knowledge and skills within these populations. Almost nothing has been committed to understanding how HRE is best accomplished in such difficult circumstances.

Human Rights Education and Peacebuilding demonstrates the promise of HRE programs to help bring about peace within challenging post-conflict contexts. Each chapter of this book (a) identifies the short and medium term impacts of seven different HRE programs on their respective target groups, and (b) provides an analysis of the peculiar local contextual factors that influenced each program's rationale for human rights education. More specifically, each chapter addresses the following critical questions:

- How are communities around the world using HRE to help rebuild their lives in the aftermath of an armed conflict?
- How does HRE respond to local problems and needs? How similar are the human rights impacts in the different projects?
- How can we understand the promise and challenges associated with HRE as a component of community peacebuilding?

This book will be of much interest to students of peacebuilding, conflict resolution, human rights, education studies, and IR in general.

Tracey Holland is Visiting Assistant Professor, Education Department, Vassar College, NY. She has a PhD in International Education from New York University.

J. Paul Martin is Director and Adjunct Professor, Human Rights Studies, Barnard College, NY, and Senior Scholar, Center for the Study of Human Rights, Columbia University, NY. He has a PhD in Comparative Education from Columbia University.

Routledge Studies in Peace and Conflict Resolution
Series Editors: Tom Woodhouse and Oliver Ramsbotham
University of Bradford

Peace and Security in the Postmodern World
The OSCE and conflict resolution
Dennis J.D. Sandole

Truth Recovery and Justice after Conflict
Managing violent pasts
Marie Breen Smyth

Peace in International Relations
Oliver P. Richmond

Social Capital and Peace-Building
Creating and resolving conflict with trust and social networks
Edited by Michaelene Cox

Business, Conflict Resolution and Peacebuilding
Contributions from the private sector to address violent conflict
Derek Sweetman

Creativity and Conflict Resolution
Alternative pathways to peace
Tatsushi Arai

Climate Change and Armed Conflict
Hot and Cold Wars
James R. Lee

Transforming Violent Conflict
Radical disagreement, dialogue and survival
Oliver Ramsbotham

Governing Ethnic Conflict
Consociation, identity and the price of peace
Andrew Finlay

Political Discourse and Conflict Resolution
Debating peace in Northern Ireland
Edited by Katy Hayward and Catherine O'Donnell

Economic Assistance and Conflict Transformation
Peacebuilding in Northern Ireland
Sean Byrne

Liberal Peacebuilding and Global Governance
Beyond the metropolis
David Roberts

A Post-Liberal Peace
Oliver P. Richmond

Peace Research
Theory and practice
Peter Wallensteen

Reconciliation after Terrorism
Strategy, possibility or absurdity?
Judith Renner and Alexander Spencer

Post-War Security Transitions
Participatory peacebuilding after asymmetric conflicts
Edited by Veronique Dudouet, Hans Giessman and Katrin Planta

Rethinking Peacebuilding
The quest for just peace in the Middle East and the Western Balkans
Edited by Karin Aggestam and Annika Björkdahl

Violent Conflict and Peacebuilding
The continuing crisis in Darfur
Johan Brosché and Daniel Rothbart

Peacebuilding and NGOs
State–civil society interactions
Ryerson Christie

Peace Negotiations and Time
Deadline diplomacy in territorial disputes
Marco Pinfari

History Education and Post-Conflict Reconciliation
Reconsidering joint textbook projects
Edited by Karina V. Korostelina and Simone Lässig

Conflict Resolution and Human Needs
Linking theory and Practice
Edited by Kevin Avruch and Christopher Mitchell

Human Rights Education and Peacebuilding
A comparative study
Tracey Holland and J. Paul Martin

Human Rights Education and Peacebuilding
A comparative study

Tracey Holland and J. Paul Martin

LONDON AND NEW YORK

First published 2014
by Routledge
2 Park Square, Milton Park, Abingdon, Oxfordshire OX14 4RN

and by Routledge
711 Third Avenue, New York, NY 10017

First issued in paperback 2015

Routledge is an imprint of the Taylor & Francis Group, an informa business

© 2014 Tracey Holland and J. Paul Martin

The right of Tracey Holland and J. Paul Martin to be identified as authors of this work has been asserted by them in accordance with sections 77 and 78 of the Copyright, Designs and Patents Act 1988.

All rights reserved. No part of this book may be reprinted or reproduced or utilized in any form or by any electronic, mechanical, or other means, now known or hereafter invented, including photocopying and recording, or in any information storage or retrieval system, without permission in writing from the publishers.

Trademark notice: Product or corporate names may be trademarks or registered trademarks, and are used only for identification and explanation without intent to infringe.

British Library Cataloguing in Publication Data
A catalogue record for this book is available from the British Library

Library of Congress Cataloging-in-Publication Data
Holland, Tracey.
  Human rights education and peacebuilding: a comparative study/Tracey Holland and J. Paul Martin.
  pages cm. (Routledge studies in peace and conflict resolution)
  Includes bibliographical references and index.
  1. Human rights–Study and teaching. 2. Peace-building. I. Martin, J. Paul. II. Title.
  JC571.H6134 2014
  323.071–dc23
                                                                2013030713

ISBN 13: 978-1-138-95191-4 (pbk)
ISBN 13: 978-0-415-82579-5 (hbk)

Typeset in Times New Roman
by Wearset Ltd, Boldon, Tyne and Wear

Contents

Preface x
Acknowledgments xiii

Introduction 1
Peacebuilding *1*
Human rights education: mandates and frameworks *1*
Moving from the universal to the particular and addressing praxis *4*
Introducing the studies *6*
Methodology *8*
Data collection and analysis *9*
Significance *10*
How to use this book *11*

1 **Mobilizing to change the status of women: a rights education project in Sierra Leone** 14
The conflict in Sierra Leone *14*
The need for grassroots human rights education *15*
The African Human Rights Education Project *16*
Assessing the impacts *18*
Challenges *23*
Conclusion *24*

2 **Melel Xojobal: addressing the rights of child workers in Chiapas, Mexico** 26
Introduction *26*
The children of Chiapas *27*
The origin of Melel's Human Rights Education Project *28*
Melel's educational approach *30*
Efficacy as the heart of Melel's Human Rights Education Program *33*

    Assessment of learning and the challenges ahead 36
    Conclusion 37

3 Education to address violence against women in rural Peru   38
    Introduction: Institute for Legal Defense's history of human rights education 38
    Cusco: violence against women and limited access to justice in rural areas 40
    The IDL community defenders and the human rights education training 42
    The impact of the IDL-CD's human rights education approach 45
    Conclusion 50

4 Human rights education in a secondary school in a conflict-torn region of Senegal   52
    The conflict in Casamance 52
    The role of human rights education in building peace 53
    The Human Rights Education Program at Malick Fall 55
    The program's significance as a means of promoting children's educational and civic participation 57
    Impact assessment: critical thinking, empathy, and civic responsibility 59
    Sustainability 62
    Conclusion 63

5 Never again: the Master's degree in human rights in Lima, Peru   65
    The conflict and the Institute 65
    The core components of the Master's degree in human rights 67
    Impact assessment 72
    The challenges 73
    Future direction: distance learning 74
    Conclusion 75

6 Addressing the causes of conflict: human rights education in Liberia   77
    The conflict in Liberia 77
    Introducing human rights education 78
    The work of the Rights and Rice Foundation in the Foya District of Liberia 79
    The Human Rights Education Program 81

Assessing human rights education's impact 84
Challenges 87
Conclusion 89

7 **The City of Women in Cartagena, Colombia, a human rights community of practice** 92
   The conflict in Colombia 92
   The League of Displaced Women 93
   The City of Women 95
   Findings: empowerment and human rights education as an act of resistance 97
   Impact assessment: the City of Women as a human rights community of practice 99
   Implications for human rights education 100
   Future directions 101

Conclusion: human rights education and peacebuilding—promises, challenges, and outcomes 103
   The promise 103
   Findings on the impact of human rights education 105
   Human rights education, culture, and peacebuilding 106
   What have we learned about outreach and sustainability? 108
   Human rights education and peacebuilding: challenges and opportunities 110

Bibliography 113
Index 121

Preface

Human rights education (HRE) offers not just a vision of human dignity but also a set of internationally agreed-upon legal principles that individuals, communities, and social movements can abide by and invoke as they seek to rebuild societies by encouraging their members to revere tolerance, display respect, and continually work toward the goal of equality. Most scholars and human rights practitioners now agree that even short-term HRE programs can make communities aware of their human rights and thereby empower them to preserve and expand such rights, both their own and the rights of their fellow citizens. They also agree that when the learning is widespread, the broader peacebuilding agenda stands a better chance of taking hold. The good news is that we can now see emerging, as an effective tool for furthering democracy and rebuilding post-conflict societies all around the world, a human rights education that is interactive and change-oriented, but nonetheless firmly rooted in the international conventions and declarations, domestic laws and constitutions that are intended to safeguard human rights.

This book is designed to look closely at HRE in a particular context, namely post-conflict peacebuilding. Its aim is to inspire, teach, and inform HRE planners, policy-makers, and practitioners who work on peacebuilding. We believe that the real promise of HRE is yet to be realized. As part of peacebuilding HRE is the one activity that gives citizens at large the chance, and some of the tools necessary to address behaviors that foment unrest, discord, and anxiety at the grassroots level. More specifically, as these chapters demonstrate, through human rights education people can learn (a) to set common goals and collaborate with one another and (b), what the responsibilities of the government are, and (c) to make claims upon that government and upon those who have the power to enact change at the local level. The skills imparted by the HRE programs depicted in this book help people to gain access to justice, to work with and through political institutions, to fight all forms of discrimination and exclusion, and to rethink any and all social factors that may have prompted the human rights abuses of the recent past. Most notably these HRE programs have sought to find ways to reduce those gender-aggravated human rights violations that already existed, but that also increased during times of conflict, and that continue even now that the conflicts are officially over.

Throughout its chapters the reader will find numerous, vivid examples of the impact that HRE has had on people in real-world situations, from women displaced by violence, to high school students and their teachers, to children working in the streets, to lawyers and social workers, to tribal chiefs in transitional, post-conflict communities within Colombia, Liberia, Mexico (Chiapas), Peru (Lima and Cusco), Senegal (Casamance) and Sierra Leone. Although each of these places has its own unique characteristics and experiences with peacebuilding, four similarities can be pointed to, as characterizing the lives of their citizens. First, people are simply trying to put their lives back together after their homes and communities have been torn apart by conflict. In most cases this means they have been displaced from their homes and former land holdings, or they have returned to ones that need to be rebuilt. Second, the people in the programs we studied find themselves caught up in a dire economic situation characterized by food and shelter insecurity. Third, the participants in the HRE programs we studied faced substantial discrimination and structural violence, with most of it being linked to ethnic status, to being a woman, or to both of these factors. Fourth, the children and young people in these communities which might not have experienced direct hostilities still see themselves as without much of a future. All of these people experience daily violations of their economic, social, cultural and political rights. In some cases, such as the Colombian one, the people we studied still face direct threats not just to their well-being, but to their lives.

In all of these places the educators and their target populations, especially women, see education as a tool of social change. The people in our studies perceive human rights as one of the ways they can address their problems. Thus what ties education together with human rights is the hope they jointly evoke from many people: that education will transform the unjust conditions they face by elevating their rights-consciousness and enabling them to become agents. However, the reality is that enormous obstacles still have to be overcome before meaningful social changes can take place. First there are the physical challenges—above all a lack of infrastructure and of resources—which remind us that human rights education is not a stand-alone activity. Future conflicts could well be averted by bringing poor communities immediate improvement with respect to water, sanitation, clinics, schools, and roads. But while the physical challenges are great, the psychological and social challenges are even greater. The social conflicts that have broken out in these places have fomented suspicions by breaking down trust among individuals and between communities. In addition to distrust between neighbors, a sense of powerlessness also afflicts those living within, or in the aftermath of, a social conflict. Thus human rights educators must show and even prove to those they are working with, that domestic and international human rights laws really do empower them to demand that government officials provide the services so essential to rebuilding and sustaining their communities. It must provide learners with the requisite conceptual and practical tools to rebuild their human relationships and to address the causes of the fissures that had opened up in their communities.

Human rights instruction also gives an individual the skills and knowledge to stand up not only to public officials, most notably members of the military and the police, but also to traditional leaders, teachers, spouses, and all others who stand between them and their basic human rights and freedoms. Further, many conflicts can be traced back to large-scale discrimination imposed by one tribe or group or class upon another. Such discrimination remains an obstinate cause of human rights abuses, and thus an underlying obstacle to the realization of HR and the subsequent empowerment of vulnerable populations. While virtually everyone can see the major role frequently played by broad-based discrimination in fomenting violent conflict, peace-builders, and HR educators are able to see it persisting even after the external violence itself has ceased. Throughout this book the reader will see how human rights educators seek to extirpate discrimination, particularly against women and children. One of the chief purposes of HRE in peacebuilding settings is to address racial, ethnic, gender and age-discrimination.

Acknowledgments

This volume would not have been possible without the contributions of many people and institutions. It grew out of two research grants we received from the United States Institute of Peace (USIP). The first research project, in 1999–2000, was based at the Center for the Study of Human Rights at Columbia University. Our reporting format was a handbook entitled *Never Again: The Case for Civic and Human Rights Education to Prevent Future Conflicts*, which in the early 2000s came to be used by UN peacekeeping missions and humanitarian and relief organizations in several countries.

Recognizing that the peacebuilding field was deficient in systematic research, the USIP granted us, in 2009, a second award to return to the field for further study. This facilitated face-to-face exchanges with the educators and researchers whose insights into HRE appear in this book. These individuals were chosen because of their familiarity with the social, political, and cultural problems associated with human rights learning in societies emerging from civil conflict. Our analysis has been immeasurably enriched by these collaborators' specialized knowledge of both the local conditions and specific problems facing their communities and the efforts of the local human rights educators. We would like to acknowledge them formally in this section.

In Sierra Leone we wish to acknowledge the work of Morrison Saidu. His assistance has been invaluable, in opening to us the doors of the project he directed, the African Human Rights Education Project in Sierra Leone. In order to collect the information that is presented in Chapter 1, Morrison traveled to six communities in Western Sierra Leone where the AHRE has been operating since 2010. We drew upon Morrison's expertise in participatory methodologies, human rights, and non-literate communities, as we slowly teased out the actual impacts of the project on the educators and community members who have been involved with the AHRE. Indeed, we also would like to thank the community leaders whom Moisa interviewed.

In Chiapas, Mexico, we collaborated with Lucie Nečasová, who in 2010 was doing her doctoral research exploring the changes in the lives of women in two communities in Lacanjá Chansayab, and Nahá, in the Lacandon jungle region of Chiapas. She took time away from her research to study Project Melel, and thus it is Lucie whom we must thank for identifying Melel as the best subject for this case, and for realizing that the best approach to data collection would be that she volunteer at Melel and engage directly with the children. She collected their drawings and conducted extensive interviews with Melel staff and other children's rights directors in Chiapas. Her detailed commentary of the impact of the HRE on the children, as revealed through their drawings and the interviews, as well as background information about Chiapas, is available in Spanish upon request. We also have greatly benefited from the insights of the current Melel director, Patricia Figueroa, as well as from her instructors and young students. Finally, this study would not have come to fruition had it not been for the support of Dr. José Luis Escalona Victoria, a scholar of the Tojolabal communities in Chiapas and the Regional Director of CIESAS Southeast.

With respect to our study of the Community Defenders or *Defensorías Comunitarias* of Cusco, Peru, we are grateful for the support of the Instituto de Defensa Legal (IDL). We are especially grateful to Christine Benoît, who had been working at IDL since 2002 and who, at the time of our research in 2010, was heading a project devoted to giving rural women access to justice in Cusco. The assistance of Aarón Verona Badajoz was also invaluable. At the time of our study he was serving as a paralegal at the Instituto de Defensa Legal in Lima, working in the area of justice system reform. Chapter 3 in this book draws on the data that Christine and Aaron collected and analyzed in a background paper written in Spanish for this research project.

Our research on the CIVITAS project in Senegal, presented in Chapter 4, owes much to Aminata Dieye, who like Morrison has served as the director of AHRE in Senegal. Our findings draw on her extensive human rights experience, both internationally and in Senegal—most notably her founding of the Rencontre Africaine pour la Défense des Droits de l'Homme (RADDHO) and her service with the African Commission and the African Union. Not only did Aminata steer us to the Malick Fall school as an important HRE model, she also created and implemented the research methodology that uses poetry and drawings to elicit from the students their ideas about human rights. Her insistence that we get in touch with alumni of the Citizen Action Program (CAP) at Malick Fall led us to our conclusion that the impact of the project is not being sustained after the students graduate. We also wish to acknowledge the contributions of the teachers themselves. Their interviews with Aminata have been recorded and transcribed, and are available upon request from the authors.

In Lima, Peru, we wish to acknowledge Professor Elizabeth Salmón, both the Coordinator of the M.A. program in Human Rights and the Director of the Institute for Democracy and Human Rights (IDEH), and Mariana Chacón Lozano, the Assistant Coordinator of the M.A. program in Human Rights and the Institute for Democracy and Human Rights. Both Elizabeth and Mariana participated in this research project, enabling us to conduct interviews, to sit in on classes, and to review documentation about the MA program.

In Liberia we collaborated with James Yarsiah, who since 2007 has served as the executive director of the Rights and Rice Foundation (RRF) which we discuss in Chapter 6. Patience Lardner, an HRE trainer for RRF, traveled to Lofa

County in the Foya District, where RRF works with many communities. In various locations, Patience ran focus-group interviews with community members who had benefitted from RRF's work. We are very grateful to James and Patience for allowing us to examine their HRE project, and to James especially for organizing the interviews and providing us with background information on the Liberian political context.

In Colombia we were fortunate to have an opportunity to study the League of Displaced Women, a Cartagena-based non-governmental organization led by Patricia Guerrero. Chapter 7 relies on research done in the spring of 2010 by the Colombian educator Paula Ramírez Diezgranados. A Peace-Educator with UNOY, she traveled to Cartagena to visit the site of the City of Women and to interview its leaders and some of the women of the League. We rely heavily on Paula's reporting and analysis in Chapter 7. We have been inspired by her depiction of a community of women highly committed to implementing a rights-based social order.

In addition to these collaborators, we also wish to express our deep indebtedness to those students at Vassar College who have worked on this project: Sharon Freiman, Mario Sosa, Ellen Butler, Sarah New, Nate McNamara, and Katie Torrisi. Special mention needs to be made of our colleague, Tania Bernath, whose field experience in post-conflict Africa emphasized feasibility and action, not just analysis and good ideas.

Introduction

> Human rights education can be defined as education, training and information aimed at building a universal culture of human rights. A comprehensive education in human rights not only provides knowledge about human rights and the mechanisms that protect them, but also imparts the skills needed to promote, defend and apply human rights in daily life. Human rights education fosters the attitudes and behaviors needed to uphold human rights for all members of society.
>
> (United Nations, World Programme for HRE 2006: 6)

Peacebuilding

The context for these studies of human rights education is that of the broader view of peacebuilding, namely one that extends beyond the formal international missions initiated by the United Nations and other regional organizations. Thus conceived human rights education is one of a number of potential peacebuilding components. Among the others are the security operations mounted by national and international military and police units, the demobilization and disarmament of former combatants, the range of other human rights activities associated with truth, reconciliation and transitional justice, the national and international activities designed to support the rebuilding of the national government, its ministries, institutions and social services, as well as other activities directed towards re-establishing the national economy. Within this complex, human rights education is typically unique because it alone focuses on the daily lives of the citizenry at large. Moreover, it is also most likely to be one of the few peacebuilding activities that reaches into the rural areas where human rights abuses were often most violent and the presence of government remained weak.

Human rights education: mandates and frameworks

International peace making, peace keeping and peacebuilding missions began to be promoted extensively by the international community in the early 1990s following the end of the Cold War. They were promoted primarily by the states under the auspices of the United Nations, typically through mandates devised and approved by the UN Security Council and administered under the Secretary General through the UN Department of Peace Keeping Operations (DPKO). In a 1992 document entitled *An Agenda for Peace*, the then United Nations Secretary-General Boutros-Ghali sought to develop deeper understanding and respect for the rights of minorities and respect for the needs of the more vulnerable groups of society, especially women and children. In that document human rights education was defined as a central component of peacebuilding. Shortly thereafter the UN Security Council officially voiced its support for HRE as one of many mechanisms capable of effecting institutional change in post-conflict situations. In 1993, HRE received an implicit confirmation when the Vienna Declaration and Programme of Action (VDPA) of 1993 asserted that "human rights education is essential for the promotion and achievement of stable and harmonious relationships among communities, and for fostering mutual understanding, tolerance and peace."[1]

The 2000 Brahimi Report (also referred to as the Report of the Panel on the United Nations Peace Operations) marked the completion of a commission to assess the UN's peacekeeping and peacebuilding activities. It urged a greater effort to ensure that the promulgation of human rights became an integral part of peacekeeping and especially peacebuilding missions,[2] calling for dedicated human rights, gender, and child-protection units to be included within all civilian missions. Human rights education did indeed become a component of some UN peacebuilding missions following the Brahimi Report, but had been used earlier, such as in Cambodia in 1992. In the field, however, these new education mandates often were implemented without sufficient forethought and planning. In Liberia, for example, the human rights unit of the peacebuilding operation numbered around 50 international personnel but only one had an education mandate. The others specialized in collecting evidence of past human rights abuses.[3]

During the first decade of the twenty-first century, the field of post-conflict practices and peacebuilding benefited from the introduction of various transitional-justice mechanisms, including national truth commissions whose findings often recommended increased HRE. Peacebuilding also saw the introduction and increased use of international criminal justice procedures as well as an emphasis on rule of law and local processes to assure the accountability for past human rights abuses. Many national peace and reconciliation commissions were established in an effort to move beyond the conflicts. A number of these national human rights commissions provided the impetus for human rights education. Among them was the Truth and Reconciliation Commission (TRC) of Peru. Its 2001 report recommended the implementation of human rights instruction at all levels.[4] As a result, in 2006 the Catholic University of Peru, in Lima, created the country's first-ever Master's Program in Human Rights. In Liberia, the Truth and Reconciliation Commission's final report of 2009 called for human rights education.[5] The Independent National Commission on Human Rights was then formed to ensure that, among other provisions, human rights education would be widely implemented in Liberian society. Thereafter, the Liberian government, as well as groups working within national, non-governmental human rights movements, have been holding training workshops in human rights.

The purpose of this book is to investigate how the calls made by the Brahimi Report, the Agenda for Peace, and the Vienna Declaration for Human Rights Education as a part of peacebuilding have been carried out, and in this case, how they have reached the more vulnerable groups, most notably women and girls. In Sierra Leone for example, in 2002, the national government signed up to various international human rights treaties. It then passed, and began to implement the Child Rights Act of 2007[6] which was modeled on the United Nations Convention of the Rights of the Child (CRC),[7] as well as the Three Gender Laws of Sierra Leone. These domestic legal instruments are consistent with the priority recommendations of the report of its Truth and Reconciliation Commission,[8] which were submitted to the government of Sierra Leone as part of the Commission's effort to improve the lives of women and girls. The head of the African Human Rights Education Project (AHREP) in Sierra Leone could then set two goals for HRE in that post-conflict context: "We need human rights education now more than ever, to tackle the discrimination against women and to enforce the implementation of these international treaties of protection and fulfillment of their human rights" (telephone interview, Moisa Saidu, October 2010).

In the field of HRE the NGOs are important actors on account of their access to funding, expertise, and for their people mobilization skills. In Sierra Leone, for instance, as well as in other African nations, Amnesty International national sections developed the African Human Rights Education Project to bring human rights education to local urban and rural communities. These projects partner community groups in teaching human rights and developing localized human rights-related projects.[9] With support from such projects some local teachers and schools in Africa and elsewhere have begun to incorporate HRE into their permanent curricula and have worked with such UN programs as UNICEF and UNESCO to implement HRE. Human rights NGOs have been especially persistent in promoting popular education, in the state of Chiapas, Mexico. HRE programs funded by outside groups such as the one at the school Malick Fall in the conflict-affected Casamance region, are building on Senegalese educators' interest to bring human rights education into their nation's schools.

Today human rights educators working within peacebuilding have gained greater leverage on account of the widespread adoption by member states of human rights education as proposed in two important UN programs: the World Decade for Human Rights Education (1995–2005)[10] and the World Program for Human Rights Education.[11] The first phase of the World Program, originally planned for 2005–2007 and later extended through 2009, focused on human rights education in primary and secondary schools. The second phase, 2010–2014, and thus ongoing at the time of this book's publication, focuses on HRE in higher education. This second phase also urges the provision of specialized HRE training for teachers and educators, civil servants, law-enforcement officials, and military personnel.[12] In Senegal and in other countries the UN initiatives have given national HRE planners a sense of solidarity and direction by delineating human rights education as a field of inquiry capable of standing on its own, apart from such other educational frameworks as civic education and peace education. It has also given impetus to national human rights educators to "provide a concrete framework for action and to strengthen partnerships and cooperation from the international level down to the grassroots."[13] National human right governments have been obligated to support training programs in human rights for teachers, other civil servants, members of security forces, and justice officials.

These frameworks make a brief yet explicit reference to the role HRE is expected to play within peacebuilding programs: "Human rights education contributes to the long-term prevention of human-rights abuses and violent conflicts."[14] This language has brought credibility and legitimacy to the work of human rights educators around the world. It has been reinforced by more general documents on education and human rights with reference to women and children issued by both UNICEF and UNESCO.

With these international documents and policies in place, and with the backing of the various national peace and reconciliation commissions, the question asked by this book is what does human rights education look like viewed from the grassroots, namely from the point of view of the rural and urban communities that are emerging from years of violence. It is the conviction of the authors that the relationship between peacebuilding and human rights education has yet to be fully analyzed, let alone utilized in mandates and mission planning. Even as the aforementioned mandates, initiatives, and HRE programs make headway, and a broader movement of human rights education gathers momentum, there remains a disconnect between the potential sources of funding—governments, NGOs, and other outside groups—and the programs themselves. To put the problem more bluntly, while governments and government officials have paid plenty of lip service to international human rights doctrine, for the most part they have done so without committing the funding needed to create stable and sustainable peacebuilding programs at the level of ordinary citizens, including those who live in rural areas and have been most abused by the previous, and sometimes still ongoing, violence.

Moving from the universal to the particular and addressing praxis

> Effective human rights education "[s]hall be shaped in such a way as to be relevant to the daily lives of the learners, and shall seek to engage learners in a dialogue about the ways and means of transforming human rights from the expression of abstract norms to the reality of their social, economic, cultural and political conditions."[15]

The educators participating in this international study recognize the need to transform international universal rights into domestic law in the form of legal, political, social, cultural, and economic claims and entitlements adapted to local culture and resources. Only when that framework is more established, known, accessible, and enforceable in law will marginalized and vulnerable individuals and groups be empowered to obtain their rights and remedy any abuses. Implicit in this process is the empowerment of disenfranchised or violence ridden communities through education and capacity building in human rights discourse and process in such a way that it is meaningful for people. In this work, HRE programs derive their rationales, goals, and strategies from the specific environment of their target communities. Their instruction and training must be relevant to the daily lives of the people and they must use a language which builds on their concepts of rights and justice. These principles are very much in keeping with the ideas of the human rights scholars Abdi and Shultz (2008) who argue that if the established universal approaches to human rights are to be effective, rights must be interpreted locally and tailored to specific situations.

This book builds on the established theory and practice of human rights education, notably through the use of three central pedagogical tenets: vernacularization or local relevance, practical application or action oriented learning, and transformative outcomes. We use all three tenets—local relevance, action-oriented learning or engagement, and the transformative impacts—as lenses through which we examine the seven cases. We are especially concerned with the third tenet, namely identifying the ways in which a community was transformed by the education.

The first tenet is that HRE must be presented in ways that promote open and free debate and thereby transform into local knowledge and culture, broader concepts about rights, justice, and development. For Mayan children in Chiapas, Mexico, this vernacularization takes the form of contextualizing children's rights by relating them to the Totzil concept of *Lekil Kuxlejal*, "a good life."

The second tenet of human rights education is that we must study and teach it in "praxis"—that is, in relation to its ability to engage individuals in action in their daily lives. This book highlights HRE's power to help people work out concrete solutions to pressing problems, and to open up spaces of social and educational change that allow under-represented groups to make rights-claims that they previously could not. In some of our cases, human rights are literally enacted, via community-theater. In other cases human rights action takes the form of children conducting research in their communities so as to highlight the most pressing needs and bring them to the attention of government officials. This kind of action has included women in Colombia building homes that provide them with shelter and stability, which has in turn allowed them to engage more thoughtfully and critically with the issues related to human rights and violence against women in their communities. Action engages the mind and the body of the learner in ways that are especially conducive to long-term assimilation of the content of what is being taught. It also makes learners contextually aware of the fact that their own, and the rights of others, can be secured only when they fully commit themselves physically and mentally, to the process of obtaining them. This process empowers and liberates the people by providing them with the tools that allow their communities to self-advocate (Baxi 1994).

The third tenet of human rights education relates to its impact: HRE must have some transformative power on people's lives. There are many ways to define and measure transformations in peoples' lives. In the case of communities recovering from conflict, their lives and circumstances have already been changed and there is a decided sense in all the communities we studied that there is no going back. What is in question is the direction of transformation in the future. In human rights terms this means the educators must help the communities to establish conditions that offer greater freedom, respect, nonviolence, and the conditions necessary for economic well-being and peace. Thus to fight violence, the educators in Liberia helped communities establish their own community groups whereas those in Cusco, Peru urged the communities to use the court system. The educators were also afraid that any changes would not be sustainable, and that any positive effects would be short-lived once they left, or the funds ran out.

While some critics of the international human rights community complain that human rights are ideals that exist merely on paper or apply only to communities with a certain culture or at a particular stage in development, the studies in this book show that as communities recover from years of violence, human rights education programs enable them to use the theoretical notion of human rights as tools to address the particular problems of their locales and communities. Quite simply, the experiences described in this book reveal how educators were able to bridge the gap between the human rights contained in official documents and the real-world needs and anxieties of people living within post-conflict contexts. This was particularly true in virtually all the studies with respect to violence against women. In these cases the violence so de-stabilized the community that women used the opportunity to address their own and their children's long-standing experience as victims of domestic violence.

Introducing the studies

These studies grew organically out of earlier research on human rights education in post-conflict zones by the same authors, through which we were able to identify the particular educational components of human rights education adapted to meet the needs of communities recovering from civil conflict. This book builds on the earlier study by looking more closely at the impact of the educators' work. We did not try to seek common indicators of impact because the seven studies had different goals and target groups as well as different social and physical conditions and histories. The one striking common denominator, however, was the degree to which all seven studies provided evidence of the embedded nature of domestic and systemic violence against women which was then aggravated during each of the conflicts.

The first chapter examines the African Human Rights Education Project, in Sierra Leone, West Africa. The focus of the project was on women, and more particularly on breaking the longstanding chain of control and cruelty that the women of that nation have experienced at the hands of the patriarchal authorities—chiefs, fathers, brothers, and husbands. Family matters had, until recently, been deemed strictly private and hence beyond the scope of the public realm of governmental authority and intervention. To begin to remedy this situation, human rights education programs were organized by the educators. The programs sought to overcome the institutionalization of the public–private dichotomy by implementing human rights training that embraced inclusionary approaches to human rights and by incorporating the women's own diverse experiences into the educational methodologies.

Our research on the work of the organization Melel Xojobal in Chiapas, Mexico, has led us to focus in the second chapter on the many children of San Cristóbal de las Casas who work on the streets and suffer from extreme poverty, random violence, and a dearth of social opportunities. Melel Xojobal has been instrumental in educating child workers and their families about their human rights, especially the rights to ethnic and linguistic identity, education, healthcare, freedom of information and expression, and protection against various forms of mistreatment. Although this organization is bringing children and their families some understanding of their rights and causing them to advocate for change, we will see that more efforts are required from others if the children's lives are to be more fully transformed.

The third chapter explores the Community Defenders Project sponsored by the Legal Defense Institute (IDL) and which is designed to bring human rights education and access to justice to the people of Cusco, Peru. Our study grows out of the 2004 Peruvian Truth and Reconciliation Commission's Final Report, which identified a need to dramatically upgrade the access of citizens to formal justice and security, especially in rural areas. The chapter demonstrates how women's participation in the education program has allowed them to gain a sense of the benefits conferred by Peruvian citizenship, more confidence in their ability to respond to problems, and sharper skills in the area of critical self-reflection.

The fourth chapter examines the Citizen Action Program (CAP) provided by the organization CIVITAS-Senegal at the Malick Fall School in Casamance, Senegal. Here we show how the implementation of an HRE program at this school led to changes in the teachers' and students' understanding of their daily experiences at school, in the community, and its surrounding institutions. Thus they embodied the principles they had learned about, those implicit within the various articles of the international human rights documents they had studied.

In the fifth chapter we explore the Master's Program in Human Rights that is provided by the Pontifical Catholic University of Peru (PUCP) in Lima. The goal of the program is to cultivate in its graduate students, the knowledge and skills they can use to promote human rights in their ensuing professional work. The impact of this program was measured through interviews with those students, which showed that most graduates had indeed gone on to teach others about human rights.

The sixth chapter looks at HRE component of the Peacebuilding and Reconciliation Project (PRP) in the Foya District of Lofa County, Liberia. On the basis of the needs-assessment carried out by the leaders of the PRP who work under the aegis of the Rights and Rice Foundation (RRF) a decision was made to devote their time and resources to building up the capacity of local Community Peace Committees (CPCs), entities specifically created to adjudicate social and economic conflicts in the continuing absence of traditional government officials. In their work, the members on the various Committees underscore the need for a widespread awareness of human rights as a necessary component of any healthy community.

In the seventh chapter we examine a project run by the League of Displaced Women (LDW) in Colombia. Here we see how human rights learning takes place within the physical context of the City of Women, a community project for displaced women and their children in the municipality of Turbaco, on the outskirts of Cartagena. It is inspiring to see how women who had been victimized by their families, paramilitary forces, and drug traffickers were able to collaborate on building and maintaining homes for themselves. The women's participation in this collective life, their deep engagement with the community's activities, is itself the chief medium through which the women learn about and practice human rights.

Methodology

To select our research sites, we looked for HRE programs whose core mission was to promote a greater understanding of the human rights international conventions, treaties and declarations, as well as the national constitutions and domestic, laws intended to safeguard human rights. In all our studies, local and international laws were changing the landscape, and local groups were invoking these laws in support of their efforts. Some programs zeroed in on international human rights law while others kept their focus more national and local, but all of the educators who ran them made a point of vernacularizing human rights discourse, ensuring that the rights they were teaching were relevant to the local populations they served.

The data for this project were collected in each of the seven sites over a ten-month period in 2010. The research involved interviews, document-collection, and participant observations, plus our subsequent interpretations of all of it. In four cases, our collaborators opened their own HRE projects up to our scrutiny (Liberia-RRF, Sierra Leone-AHRE, Lima-PUCP, and Cusco-IDL). In three places (Colombia-LDW, Casamance-CAP and Chiapas-Melel), our research partners helped us to identify other HRE projects they were not affiliated with, and they conducted the interviews with personnel involved these programs. The methodology we chose was significant; with our goal of establishing connections that could have long-term impact among researchers in various nations, we chose collaborators who could write background papers of the HRE projects.

Before we selected a site for inclusion in the study, we elicited information from the director of the HRE program under consideration or from the researcher who had recommended the project for inclusion in our study by sending them a questionnaire that included these questions:

- What was the context within which the HRE program was implemented?
- Who participated in this program? Did HRE help them to address their needs? If so, how was this achieved?
- What content/teaching methods were implemented to address the learners' concerns?
- What was the intended goal of the HRE program you were associated with and/or assessed?
- What sort of human rights violations and violence characterized your country's conflict?
- Which forces helped to bring abuses to an end, and to foster social reconciliation?

On the basis of their answers we chose seven HRE programs that could best identify and describe their programs in HRE, that were consciously addressing factors associated with systemic as well as domestic violence, that would offer a different process from others in the eventual group, that worked directly with communities recovering from the violence, that addressed the problems associated with sustainability, and that had data that helped assess their respective impacts.

Data collection and analysis

In order to introduce an element of standardization into these studies of HRE in seven different peacebuilding settings, we designed research protocols that contained our principal guiding questions and worked with our research partners to adapt them to local conditions. We also arranged for all data to be sent back to us in New York using available technology, such as Skype, email, and wikis. Our research protocols sought to elicit from participants of the HRE programs (including educators and the students) their reflections on the impact that the training had had on their lives. Those protocols contained questions about any changes that had transpired within the realm of their lives. As for the educators, including community leaders or teachers who had been recipients of the HRE provided by the sponsoring organization, we wanted to know about the impact on their community-action work and how they were better equipped to handle conflict and other problems they encountered every day. In several places, the research process illuminated for local HRE directors how their and others HRE programs had proved effective in helping them to resolve conflicts in the communities in which they work. In other cases the research process and the findings fed back to the sponsoring organizations helped in the professional development of staff members both by upgrading their competence and their confidence, thereby enabling them to carry out their work at an optimal level of proficiency.

In New York we analyzed the background papers, transcripts of interview tapes, the questionnaires, and other documentation for each project, and then compared the projects with one another. We looked for common themes and insights that indicated changes in communities that had received the HRE program. Using an approach to data analysis based on the qualitative research tradition of grounded theory we selected from the questionnaires and transcriptions themes that would lead us to a better understanding of the project's impact (Auerbach 2007). We defined impact as those transformations in the lives of participants, groups or institutions that may have occurred as a result of human rights education. In each chapter we have standardized our analysis of each of the programs we studied in a way that addresses some of the chief concerns in the field, and leads our readers, students and scholars of HRE to a deeper understanding of the role HRE plays in post-conflict settings.

In keeping with the current research trend toward examining the impact of human rights programs, as well as country-specific research and policies, in their relation to historical, cultural and social contexts, the seven studies which comprise this book draw upon a broad array of sources. In addition to academic literature, our sources ranging from simple testimonials by teachers and learners—such as those one finds on the website of Africa Human Rights Education[16]—to formal evaluations that report to donors on specific projects. Our research and analyses also build upon, and extend, the existing academic research. That includes but is not limited to Tibbets' work in Romania (1999); Gervais' works on Honduras (2010) and Bolivia (2011); Marks' study of UN Peacebuilding in Cambodia (1997); and our own work Martin, Holland and Bernath (1999). The broader conclusions we have drawn, on HRE in peacebuilding, are presented in the book's final chapter.

Logistical considerations, notably limited financing, limited the geographic reach of the study, and thus we could not study the human rights education that has occurred in a wider variety of post-conflict settings. We would like to have studied HRE responses to, for example, the hate campaigns that preceded the conflicts in the Balkans, Rwanda, Darfur, Nagorno-Karabakh, Georgia/Abkhazia/South Ossetia, Israel/Palestine, and elsewhere. Investigating these and other peacebuilding contexts would have expanded our understanding of HRE's impact on peoples' lives and the ways in which it facilitates such change. Instead we have concomitantly intensified our research into the HRE that has been done in the peacebuilding contexts already well known to us.

Significance

Recent research notwithstanding, peacebuilding scholars and practitioners are still hindered by limited knowledge regarding the practice of human rights education and the resulting debates as to HRE's goals, basic components, and likely social benefits. For a variety of reasons, the international community has remained hesitant to invest its time and money in HRE. By compiling initial findings on some of the socioeconomic and political benefits presently being brought to several post-conflict societies by HRE programs, this book seeks to bolster the growing practice of human rights education and peacebuilding around the world, and thereby build confidence among donors. Beyond just motivating donors to take more action and provide more funding, however, we hope this book and its presented findings will also enable HRE planners and educators to upgrade their projects and programs.

As a contribution to the literature on human rights education, this book seeks to complement the current international monitoring of the impact of HRE upon peacebuilding efforts, which has been skewed toward legal and security perspectives, with only occasional glimpses into the surviving population's own understandings of, and responses to, the role that HRE plays in peacebuilding. For the most part, such micro-level experiences are conspicuous by their absence from most of the reports that are international in scope. Our ultimate hope is that by deepening our knowledge of the discovery and use of domestic and international human rights instruments by individual citizens, especially those in rural areas, people whose lives these standards were originally intended to protect and enhance, this book will bring both scholars and practitioners greater insights into the micro-processes of human rights learning, as those processes continue within the larger macro context of peacebuilding.

We believe that despite our relatively narrow scope, the seven stories we tell do demonstrate those aspects of local relevance, empowerment, and action-learning that jointly comprise the heart of any useful assessment of HRE's impact. Above all, the studies make it evident that human rights education can help instill confidence, enhance dignity, and augment capacity in individuals and small groups of people, and do so in ways that bring about ongoing social transformations within communities and institutions caught up in post-conflict peacebuilding and reconciliation. Practitioners and scholars alike identify such positive effects of human rights education elsewhere in the world as well.

Nevertheless, even if more resources are devoted to human rights education for communities recovering from violent civil conflict, more research is still necessary to identify the factors that best contribute to success and sustainability. The following chapters contribute to that process by examining the different answers and insights in seven communities re-building after violent conflict. The different premises and practices merit comparison both for their similarities and for their divergences. Among the cross-cutting themes we propose for comparison are:

- The quality and training of the educators
- The needs assessment and selection of target populations
- The challenges and solutions to the sustainability of both the programs and their social outcomes
- The impact of HRE on the lives of women and children
- The place of the human rights education programs as a component of domestic and international peacebuilding

How to use this book

In each chapter we describe a single program and examine the (a) expectations with respect to establishing new norms of equal rights, transparency in those rights, and individual empowerment; (b) challenges, especially the balance between the work done by outside human rights educators and by locals, engaging local officials, ensuring the sustainable success of these HRE initiatives through ongoing access to needed resources and applicability of the programs to local situations; and (c) impacts, notably HRE's capacity to empower people in post-conflict areas, reduce the tensions and violence, and raise awareness and understanding of human rights and human rights abuses in ways that lead individuals to recognize, and communities to jointly solve, the human rights-related problems plaguing their areas.

Topics that require further analysis and discussion, such as when designing new programs or instructing undergraduate and graduate students, include:

- Which are the key components that enable people around the world using HRE to help rebuild their communities, and thereby their lives in the aftermath of an armed conflict?
- What are valid critiques of human rights education? How could HRE have better served to address local problems and fulfill local needs?
- How similar is the impact of human rights across the different projects?
- How can we begin to conceptualize the promises and challenges of HRE as being intimately interconnected to community peacebuilding efforts?
- Which are the crucial social conditions, forces and institutions that strengthen or weaken the impact of HRE?

The authors look upon this book as a call to the international community to examine more closely the need for, and the benefits of, human rights education as a component of peacebuilding. However, this is not to say that all forms of human rights education are equal, or that all are effective. More studies are needed both to strengthen the case for HRE and to illustrate the costs and benefits of the different models. However it is clear to us from these studies that the quality of the different programs depends on the three criteria or tenets we identified above, namely vernacularization or local relevance, practical application or action oriented learning, and transformative outcomes. On the other hand these are not the only factors that are relevant to identifying and designing human rights education for, and with, communities emerging from violent conflict. We believe, however, that these studies offer the evidence needed to show that HRE can benefit such communities significantly, and that therefore it also ought to be an integral, not optional, component of peacebuilding. Let the reader agree or disagree.

Notes

1 www.ohchr.org/en/professionalinterest/pages/vienna.aspx.
2 The concept of "peacebuilding" became more prominent following the publication of *An Agenda for Peace* in 1992 by Boutros Boutros-Gali, former UN Secretary-General. The document created UN definitions that distinguished between "peacemaking" (action to bring hostile parties to agreement) and "peacekeeping" (a way to help

countries torn by conflict create the conditions for lasting peace), and defined "post-conflict peace-building" as "action to identify and support structures which will tend to strengthen and solidify peace in order to avoid a relapse into conflict."
3 See: Field interview, Paul Martin, (2006). www.un.org/en/peacekeeping/missions/unmil/mandate.shtml.
4 *Final report* (2001) Lima, Peru: Peruvian Truth and Reconciliation Commission (TRC) [accessed June 14, 2011], www.cverdad.org.pe/ingles/ifinal/conclusiones.php.
5 *Final report* (2008) Liberia: Truth and Reconciliation Commission of Liberia[accessed June 14, 2011], http://trcofliberia.org/reports/final-report.
6 Child Rights Act (2007). *Sierra Leone Gazette Extraordinary* CXXXVIII (43) (September 3, 2007) [accessed June 14, 2007] www.sierra-leone.org/Laws/2007–7p.pdf.
7 *Convention on the Rights of the Child* (1990). United Nations Secretary General, 44/25 [accessed June 14, 2011], http://www2.ohchr.org/english/law/crc.htm.
8 *Truth and Reconciliation Commission Act 2000* (1999) Sierra Leone: Truth and Reconciliation Commission (TRC) [accessed June 14, 2011] http://web.archive.org/web/20051230045239/www.sierra-leone.org/trcact2000.html.
9 www.amnesty.org/en/human-rights-education/projects-initiatives/ahrep.
10 United Nations General Assembly, *United Nations Decade for Human Rights Education*, A/RES/49/184. 94th Plenary Meeting sess. (December 23, 1994) [accessed June 14, 2011] www.un.org/documents/ga/res/49/a49r184.htm.
11 *Plan of action: World programme for human rights education* (2006) New York and Geneva: United Nations Educational, Scientific, and Cultural [accessed June 15, 2011] Organization; Office of the United Nations High Commissioner for Human Rights, http://unesdoc.unesco.org/images/0014/001478/147853e.pdf.
12 www2.ohchr.org/english/issues/education/training/secondphase.htm.
13 www.ohchr.org/Documents/Publications/PActionEducationen.pdf, p. 2.
14 Ibid.
15 Ibid.
16 "Africa human rights education project," in Amnesty International (2010) [accessed June 22, 2011], available at http://hreafrica.blogspot.com/; www.amnesty.org/en/human-rights-education/projects-initiatives/ahrep.

1 Mobilizing to change the status of women
A rights education project in Sierra Leone

The conflict in Sierra Leone

Sierra Leone was ravaged by civil war from 1991 until 2002. During the war an estimated 50,000 people were killed, over one million were displaced from their homes, and thousands more fell victim to brutal amputations, rapes, and assaults.[1] The chief victims of violence were civilians, not combatants. The Revolutionary United Front (RUF) rebels fomented political and institutional instability by committing massacres, burning of schools and courthouses, scattering the civilian population, and most insidiously of all, specifically targeting the chiefs—the traditional rulers in rural areas. Young RUF recruits often were deliberately sent to attack their own home villages, thereby leaving deep scars within their families and communities (Keen 2005: 60).

Even prior to the outbreak of violent civil conflict the failure of the state to provide public services and to promote economic development, had immeasurably aggravated Sierra Leone's social chaos. During the two decades preceding the 1991 outbreak, a one-party state had served the interests of a small group of the wealthy, including foreign diamond merchants, while basic social services disintegrated. As a result, in 1990 Sierra Leone had the second lowest human-development ranking in the world. Further the failure of the state to provide education and generate employment opportunities created a large pool of disenfranchised youth who felt they had little to lose by rising up violently against the system (Bellows 2006). The loss of educational opportunity is seen as a major factor in the decision to fight (Peters and Richards 1998). Women and girls also joined the conflict as fighters.

For the women and girls of Sierra Leone the war brought dreadful atrocities to their lives, especially the widespread acts of violence committed against them in all regions of the country. The human rights violations against women and children blatantly perpetrated by all groups included murder, rape, and other forms of sexual violence performed in brutal ways, sexual slavery, slave labor, abduction, assault, amputation of limbs, forced pregnancy, disembowelment of pregnant women, torture, trafficking, mutilation, theft, and the destruction of what little property they owned or rented.

In 1999, troops from the United Kingdom and the United Nations intervened and finally brought an end to the war. National elections for president and parliament were held in 2002, and local government elections were held in 2004. A reconstruction-and-reconciliation process, rife with challenges, began. The historically low status of women and the fact that so many Sierra Leoneans were made to believe that these women and girls were to blame for the violence, and that because they had been abused or violated, they were judged unworthy of respect and should not to be accepted back by their families. Attitudes like these added considerably to the challenges facing women.

In Sierra Leone today women continue to suffer from multiple forms of gender-based violence and discrimination, especially in the home. They are beaten and raped, and in some cases even killed, while many more endure psychological violence and tyrannical economic control within the home. Women who find themselves in violent relationships are often unable to leave the men on whom they and their children depend, due not only to that dependence, but also because discrimination is rampant in both education and employment and they are unlikely to find employment as a means of self-support. To compound the problem women have had little access to justice and virtually no rights within the spheres of marriage and divorce, property and inheritance. So embedded have these abuses become in the culture that even today, many men in Sierra Leone fail to see a cause for public concern in such supposedly personal matters (Maclure 2009).

The need for grassroots human rights education

The African Human Rights Education Project saw the strengthening of women's rights, and their achieving a greater participation in decision-making, as central to its task. This would mean substantial capacity building which would first confront the historical silence of women in Sierra Leone in relation to the violence which is inflicted upon them. There, as in many other countries, women are cowed into silence by a host of forces: including their own shame, fear of reprisal, fear of losing their breadwinner, and fear of being stigmatized by their communities. The most vital point here is that the culture of silence is not merely a by-product of the war; rather, it is deeply rooted in the many culture-based belief-systems that keep women and girls consistently silent. The implicit taboos against speaking out publicly in general, and in particular about the violence committed against them, make it very difficult for educators to elicit views from many women (Betancourt et al. 2010). In addition to encouraging women to speak out HRE also has to help to eradicate the deep-rooted belief that decision-making in the private and public spheres is not exclusively the province of powerful and educated men and, perhaps, the occasional woman. HR educators must not only foster the critical thinking that makes it possible for participants to reconceive that subordination but also give them, and especially the women, the skills they would need to take action.

It should be noted that the need for educators to teach human rights and address the huge challenges facing women and girls became even more pronounced after the national government signed on to various international human rights treaties. Two actions undertaken by the government after the war have been particularly significant and helpful in the eyes of human rights educators: the implementation in 2007 of the Child Rights Act (CRA), modeled upon the UN Convention on the Rights of the Child (UNCRC), and of what have become known as the Three Gender Laws of Sierra Leone: the Domestic Violence Act, the Registration of Customary Marriage and Divorce Act, and the Devolution of the Estate Act. The latter three instruments came in direct response to the priority recommendations stipulated in the Truth and Reconciliation Commission Report, with the Commission having been set up by the government of Sierra Leone as part of its effort to improve the situation of women and girls. The Domestic Violence Bill of 2007 criminalizes violence in the family, providing the police with the legal tools they need to investigate and prosecute such crimes. The Registration of Customary Marriage and Divorce Act and the Devolution of the Estate Act jointly serve to strengthen women's rights with respect to both marriage and property, thereby making it easier for them to leave abusive relationships.

This legislation also is designed to strengthen women's rights all over Sierra Leone and thereby upgrade women's social status, particularly in rural areas. The HRE community in Sierra Leone is well aware, however, that its role is to make the people aware of rights and their potential usefulness. Human rights educators also are motivated by a profound conviction that learning about their human rights allows women to radically reconceive what they used to perceive as being strictly personal problems—for example, maternal mortality—as human rights and public policy issues that affect women throughout the country. In the process of doing their consciousness-raising work, the educators and other human rights activists are learning how to use the language of international human rights law to describe the associated human rights abuses and to advocate for their victims. According to the coordinator of the African Human Rights Education Project in Sierra Leone, spreading the word about international human rights standards has simultaneously spread an awareness of the problems that plague women within their homes, and has thereby begun to break down the taboos that surround them "so we can talk about the issues openly and ultimately solve them." (Telephone interview with Moisa Saidu, October 2010).

The African Human Rights Education Project

The African Human Rights Education Project currently delivers community-level human rights education in ten countries across East and West Africa, in partnership with twenty-one local organizations.[2] The local partners mobilize community-level HRE workers and support them with the resources needed to design and deliver a range of innovative HRE projects. The project seeks to anchor a culture of human rights within specific communities, enabling people to identify local human rights issues and to connect them to human rights norms and standards. In every country where AHRE is found, one sees micro-projects in human rights education bringing their participants information on a wide range of issues including women's rights, children's rights, minority rights, economic, social and cultural rights, political violence, and maternal mortality. A central component of AHRE's strategic plan details the expectation that by training people who will then train others, the initiative will spread to many more individuals. The plan says that the micro-projects should focus on groups of 100 to 350 people.

It must also be noted that this training project and the micro-projects associated with it had to respond to, or reconcile, two mandates. The first of them sprang from the AHRE itself, a four-year project which was designed to (a) enhance civil society's capacity to deliver locally relevant human rights education, and (b) improve the human rights of the most disadvantaged by empowering marginalized communities to promote and defend their members' human rights. The term "human rights education" is carefully defined by Amnesty International as a deliberate, participatory practice aimed at empowering individuals, groups and communities through fostering knowledge, skills and attitudes consistent with internationally recognized human rights principles. The second implicit mandate was imposed by the British Government's Department for International Development (DFID). All of DFID's funded projects must promise to increase good governance and transparency by working through a variety of local partnerships and networks and by strengthening the ability of civil society and media to hold governments to account. Indeed, DFID expects all of its funded projects to improve the participants' knowledge of underlying political systems, power relationships, the role of institutions, and the dynamics of pro-poor change.

The AHRE in Sierra Leone was expressly designed to bolster the efforts of the emerging HRE community there. In February 2010, the local Amnesty International office invited fifteen human rights educators from diverse parts of Sierra Leone to participate in a three-day workshop held in the capital city of Makeni. They came from various regions of the country and represented a wide range of jobs and roles in their communities. During the workshop the participants had a chance to network and to share the new skills and knowledge about implementing human rights education that were largely drawn from the standard kit of Amnesty's HRE work. The content of the many HRE programs now being introduced into Sierra Leone conforms to the international human rights frameworks and the aforementioned national laws and policies that have incorporated them.

After the workshop in Makeni the participants returned to their home communities of Moyamba, Kenema, Kambia, and Bombali to implement various HRE micro-projects. The educators first did a needs-assessment of their respective communities, to choose one or more foci relating to HR that seemed to align with the identified needs, and designed various micro-projects that were implemented in the regions of the country. Most of the micro-projects involved the organization of discussion groups, plays and sketches, and human rights clubs—as a means to increase awareness of the human rights violations that were rampant in these communities. All of the projects were designed to bolster the status of women in these communities by addressing directly the human rights issues faced by women and children. Morrison Saidu, AHRE's national coordinator for Sierra Leone, has noted that "women living in communities have little or no knowledge of their human rights, and therefore the information and awareness provided by the micro-projects empowers them to begin to change their situations and to seek redress when violations occur" (telephone interview, October 2010). The trained educators initiated such projects armed with their knowledge of the national and international human rights laws, and the campaign that Amnesty International is currently concentrating most of its efforts on – that of maternal mortality prevention. The 15 volunteers trained in Makeni to be educators are also intended to serve as what AHRE calls "conflict mediators," trained to oversee and adjudicate the HRE efforts in their communities and well versed in effective ways to enact change that takes realistic account of likely short- and long-term impacts.

In the next section we explore the ways in which the AHRE in Sierra Leone has fulfilled its goals in the community; that is, how the Makeni training the people have received impacts their lives in their communities, and also how the educators provide information that addresses human rights violations that are occurring contemporaneously. As for the impacts, in its dictum on the measurement of any project's impact, Amnesty International speaks of "the extent to which a project or program contributes to significant changes—positive or negative, expected or unexpected—in the lives of people and communities." Impact usually takes some time to manifest itself, however; in the early stages of a project, it makes more sense to assess the "potential" for impact. Thus in our analysis of the interview data,[3] we coded for comments or anecdotes that illustrated the short-term impacts the training had on the ability of interviewees to implement in their own communities both what they had learned and the skills they had acquired—for example, inclusionary practices, community organizing, facilitating contentious discussions, and staging sketches and dramas, that bring human rights to life. We also sought to understand how the training helped educators to identify and redress human rights related problems faced by women and girls in their homes, and how to redress such violations.

Assessing the impacts

During the Makeni Workshop, the educators spent a great deal of time acquiring and honing the skills needed to lead participatory discussions about topics related to human rights. In their interviews for this study, 12 of the 15 project participants said that within four months of receiving the Makeni training they had organized at least one discussion group, play, or human rights club that led community members to mobilize women and other actors in dialogue about the human rights related issues of women.

Given the tumultuous context, the inclusion of women within discussion groups constitutes a major achievement, since historically, Sierra Leone's women and children have had no voice in decision-making at any level. These educators have gone even further, however, by getting key authority figures involved in discussions about women's rights. All of them are males, and thus the educators have sought to engage them in critique of the cultural factors that implicitly condone the perpetuation of violence against women and girls. Several of the educators interviewed about AHRE have reported success here, in that that the participatory discussions attended by several of the traditional authorities in their communities have convinced them to include women and children in various development projects, aimed at upgrading their social status and living conditions. Most notable here is the fact that the male elders in the four principal communities within the chiefdom of Nongowa have invited local women to help them establish human rights clubs in these places. Sessions of the latter will be held regularly, with the members themselves choosing the human rights related issues to be addressed.

In several communities where the micro-projects have been initiated, educators also reach out to religious authorities, primarily because the latter are in turn able to touch so many people with their messages. The results are just beginning to be felt in some places. For instance in Konta Dubalai, a village in the Kambia district, a discussion about human rights ended with a consensus on the part of community members that imams and pastors would include human rights messages in their sermons. In Grafton, in the Western Area, the Soweis, formerly some of the worst offenders when it comes to female genital mutilation/cutting (FGM), have agreed to arrest and fine any Sowei who continues to practice it in the community. The fact that the religious authorities are raising awareness about those family matters that are also vital human rights concerns is an important outcome of these discussion groups. More specifically, they are making valuable connections between HRE teachings about violations that take place in the home and pertinent passages in the Bible and the Koran.

During the Makeni workshop the participating human rights educators also received training in the use of dramatic or theater productions, as a way of raising awareness about human rights in their communities. As a result, several of the HRE micro-projects that the educators have led in their home communities have involved community theater projects. For example in all six of the mountain villages in the Western Area, educators have introduced women and children to human rights through workshops and then helped to facilitate plays and theatrical productions that address such local human rights concerns as domestic violence, the social reintegration of former child abductees, maternal mortality, and FGM. The plays have utilized as actors, local teachers, parents, girls, traditional authorities, and members of NGOs. In order to participate in this capacity, local women and children also must help to research the human rights issues that are being explored in dramatic fashion. Those explorations are in some respects quite explicit, in the sense that as opposed to leaving the underlying points merely implicit, there are moments in the plays when the other actors freeze as the protagonist asks the crowd such questions as "What are you seeing? Tell me, if it were you, what would you do?" and "What can you do to stop this from happening?" What keeps such interruptions from being too jarring is the explanation provided by an educator before the performance begins, that what is being sought is not just their verbal answers but their active participation, as human rights agents so to speak, within the flow of the drama. Music also is a vital component of such productions, given its effectiveness in conveying strong messages about social life in an emotionally charged but also inspirational way. At the end of every performance the educators elicit from the onlookers more reflection in the form of questions, comments, and suggestions, and encourage them to form human rights clubs.

Although as yet no formal study has been conducted we have seen positive outcomes associated with the use of community-theater as a means of disseminating HRE. As we have noted, both during and after the performances the audience members participate in ways that demonstrate their new understanding of the key human rights concepts and their importance. It also has been reported, albeit only second-hand in the form of anecdotal evidence, that people who had committed domestic violence prior to seeing a performance have stopped this behavior. Ultimately, though, it must be through the clubs, that the community members work out for themselves the implications of the themes that have emerged from the community plays.

The newly trained human rights educators are in an especially good position to instigate change after they have returned to their communities. Generally they are then perceived as having the requisite credentials as authorities, especially if they hold positions of higher status in their communities on account of their profession or level of higher education. A participant in the HRE program in Makeni speaks of the impact the training related to maternal mortality has had on her ability to work with those most heavily impacted by the issue:

> I am Alice Koroma. I am a Traditional Birth Attendant, and have served in the Kanthata Bana community for four years. I take care of pregnant women and of children younger than five years old, and sometimes I help to deal with general health problems. After I returned from the human rights education training, I knew much more about the causes of maternal mortality. I have held meetings in my community on how to care for and support pregnant women. So, in turn, I am sensitizing the community to consider local mechanisms, like using hammocks to transport pregnant women whose cases are urgent.

The following testimony is from another human rights educator who is a Traditional Birth Attendant as well, from the community of Mokorewo. Her words speak to the transformation she has experienced in her work, brought on by her training in human rights:

> After the workshop I came back to my village and summoned the stakeholders to share my experience. I told them that human rights have come to our community. We never knew about human rights, but good things have come to our community this year. I never knew that there is a way that one can deal with pregnant women, to deliver [babies] safely without resorting to

native herbs. Native herbs have numerous demerits: for example, they show no dosage amounts and have no expiration dates. Some native herbs are made into concoctions which have a tendency to destroy the internal organs, with overdoses leading to unanticipated abortion and even to women bleeding to death. Indeed, dependence on native herbs is one of the main causes of maternal deaths, especially in rural communities, and make no mistake, when people call for an ambulance, they certainly don't do so in the hope that native herbs will save them.

As a TBA I used to apply native herbs, but the training has led us to realize that we should stop using homegrown concoctions. Also, if we have pregnant women in our community it is our responsibility to support and care for them, to ensure that they have regular check-ups and take their pills. If you notice that a pregnant woman is not taking the advice given, you should ask the husband to support the clinic with a donation of money. The chiefs also will help by making sure the woman goes to the clinic. When you achieve this, it means you have done a good thing in the village. Human rights require that we end this practice of delivering pregnant women in the community.

A public-school teacher, John Kanga, attests to how the training he received at the Makeni workshop left him with an understanding of the situation faced by many poor girls in his village who are forced to prostitute themselves:

> During the Africa Human Rights Education workshop at Makeni, I learned a lot of things in connection with the Child Rights Act, such as teenage pregnancy and maternal mortality. These problems are very severe in our community due to its abject poverty. Most of the school-age girls hail from very poor homes, where their parents don't have the money to support their education. As a solution the girls will resort to anything, including latching onto older men, to get money to solve their social problems. Their connections with these men lead to teenage pregnancy. Many girls are then left alone to have their babies. At the end of the day they can't deliver the baby themselves; they experience obstruction, and die in the process. In many cases, the babies don't survive either.

The HRE workshop has made these community leaders aware that such issues are human rights issues and that they have an obligation to identify and report them, and to follow up on them in court. Further, John has gained knowledge about human rights that he now feels a moral obligation to share with his students. He believes that even the men of Sierra Leone are now, however, feeling the need to subscribe to the new ways of seeing and acting. John's efforts to teach his students about the mechanisms now protecting and promoting the rights of women in Sierra Leone, would have little hope of succeeding, however, were he not aware that he himself can invoke the Child Rights Act (CRA), enacted by the Sierra Leonean government in 2007. He now can forcibly convey the fact that when older men take in young girls and provide them with food and shelter in return for sex, they are committing a human rights violation in the eyes both of their own government and of the world. Here a young teenage pupil at the primary school in Mokorewo shares what she has learned from John:

> We learned about children's rights during the workshop [given by Mr. Kanga]: we have the right to an education; we have a right to life; we have a right to eat; we have right to study. If our parents send us to school, we should go to school and not to the men.

That casual reference to "the men," as an alternative destination instead of school, reminds us just how important it is that these women learn how to stand up for their rights. Only in that way can they break the pernicious trends whereby girls get money, food, and shelter from older men in exchange for sex. Next, another teacher's story eloquently attests to the impact that human rights education has had on her ability to advocate for a child in her class:

> Mariama was twelve when her father passed away. Two years later her father's younger brother, (also called her "junior father") took her to live with him in his house, together with his two sons. During this period he slept in the same bed with Mariama. He said this was the only way to prove he cared, and to protect her. As any child would, she thought that through such sentiments he was proving his love for her, as her father had done when he had been alive. One day, however, he led the girl by the hand into a bedroom and said that he wanted to see whether she had been tampered with by men. He tied her hands and stuffed her mouth with a piece of cloth. He raped her and threatened that if she told anyone, he would kill her. He continued this game till the poor girl became pregnant.
>
> In school, Mariama would sleep through each class. As her teacher, I often noticed her not cooperating in class and consistently sleeping, so I decided to ask what the matter was. She told me she was fine, but as a parent myself, I was suspicious. I insisted that something must be wrong, and that she should open up to me. Finally she did so, and in the course of sharing the full story with me she said she had been threatened by her junior father at home.
>
> What I learned from the HRE workshop that I attended earlier this year is that all such matters must be reported to the police, and the perpetrator must be brought to justice. The fact that he is a girl's junior father does not give him the right to rape her. Such issues have been prevalent in our communities for far too long, but they have been constantly kept under the table in the name of culture but also because we did not know that they constitute serious crimes, as we have now been taught. The HRE workshop has made us aware that such issues are human rights issues and that we have an obligation to identify and report them, and to follow up on them in court.

When you educate us, you are giving us the knowledge to take the necessary action that we would not have taken otherwise.

In all of these examples we have heard community leaders, including professionals, attest to how their incorporation of human rights into their thinking about their work has provoked them to take a hard new look at those traditional cultural practices that do violence, both physical and spiritual, to Sierra Leone's young girls and women. While we cannot yet form a deeper analysis of how these professionals are applying human rights to their respective jobs, we do see the short-term impacts the training had on the interviewees' ability to implement in their own communities both what they had learned, and the skills they had acquired that bring human rights to life. Clearly, the Makeni training has a positive impact in establishing a new social precedent, that of placing a new, higher premium on the lives of the nation's women and girls.

Challenges

In this chapter we have been examining just the initial positive impacts that the newly trained HRE workers have brought back to their communities, several months after their training. That assessment more broadly reveals, however, that human rights education can open up spaces within which long marginalized groups such as women can feel sufficiently free and empowered to speak and take action. We also have seen educators and activists accomplishing what would have been seen as an insurmountable task in the past; namely, including traditional authorities and religious figures in their discussions about how to upgrade the status of women and children and how to punish those who violate their rights, even when the violators are men and thus traditionally more dominant.

Inevitably, many challenges remain. Most broadly, the human rights educators in Sierra Leone who have had notable success in engaging women in dialogue, must increasingly build upon the women's heightened awareness to help them bring about concrete changes in their own and their fellow citizen's lives. At this stage in the peacebuilding process, the AHRE project is designed to teach women and children what their rights are, and to ensure that others recognize that many violations of women's rights are taking place in the homes of Sierra Leone. As knowledge of their rights increases, women need to upgrade their ability to demand accountability on the part of those who are now legally obligated to protect those rights. It is not enough just to tell their constituents that a particular action constitutes a human rights violation; they also must teach them *why* it is a violation and, above all, what they can do about it. That real progress is being made in this area is attested to by the many educators who told us that participants in their HRE project no longer merely demand their rights in a vacuum; they also want to be able to invoke the relevant international and locally enforceable documents and standards that protect and promote those rights.

A second challenge relates to sustainability. While human rights workers in Sierra Leone are highly motivated to continue their work they are daunted by difficulties ranging from limited coordination and collaboration with other human rights educators to a lack of space and time, within which they can evaluate previous work and share results. The ultimate goal, however, must be to make sure that these projects continue to have ongoing support from Amnesty International, for without that, none of the education projects on national and local levels will be sustainable. Amnesty International must also decide whether they want to teach the participants more about the national and international human rights laws pertaining to the issue (e.g. in Makeni it was maternal mortality) that Amnesty International is currently concentrating most of its efforts, or also to raise other rights issues faced by women that fall outside the scope of the official campaigns.

The attitude of Sierra Leone's national government presents a third major challenge. Although it has enacted policies and legal instruments modeled upon international human rights frameworks, human rights educators lack concrete policies and practices that assure the day-to-day protection of women and children and increase their levels of civic participation. Above all, and as John Kanga noted earlier, abject poverty remains a terrible reality in the lives of so many people in Sierra Leone, thereby intensifying the misery of the many women and children. The emerging awareness of the human rights possessed by all, most importantly by women and children, will not be sustainable unless it is accompanied by measures to alleviate poverty.

Conclusion

In Sierra Leone and many other countries, much of the violence against women occurs in the private, non-governmental sphere, in their homes and in their communities. In that private family realm, women's rights are violated in many ways, from physical violence to coercion in decision-making and the allocation of work and other responsibilities. These violations take place outside the public sphere and have therefore been construed not to be privy to government and government officials. Worldwide, the violation of women's rights has also had a considerable impact on who can participate fully and effectively in the public spheres of politics, civil society, and markets (Bunch 1990: 13). There is evidence in our analysis of the AHRE program in Sierra Leone showing that rights violations can be brought into the public realm through discussion groups, clubs, theater performances, and through the work of professionals. International and national human rights laws help to support these micro-level initiatives and the creation of a public culture around violations that used to be concealed. The ongoing process of human rights education is beginning to bring women's issues out of the darkness of ignorance and fear while exposing them through the increasingly transparent public, legal domain, and placing them within the scope of governmental authority and intervention. By implementing inclusionary and participatory approaches to human rights education, and by reaching out to communities and government officials in order to spread the various messages, the first and foremost task that members of the HRE community working in Sierra Leone are accomplishing is that of undermining the regressive institutionalization of the public-private dichotomy.

Notes

1 www.hrw.org/reports/1999/sierra/.
2 The AHRE project is a project being implemented in ten West and East African countries: Benin, Burkina Faso, Côte d'Ivoire, Ghana, Kenya, Mali, Sierra Leone, Senegal, Togo, and Uganda.
3 In order to collect data for this case study, interviews were conducted in ten communities with 15 project participants roughly five months after they had received their Makeni training, during the months of January and February, by a researcher who had received training in recording testimonies, Through these interviews the research acquired a sense of the emerging impact of the micro-projects, their successes and setbacks, and how well the newly trained HR educators had been able to adapt what they had learned in their training workshops to their work in the community. All these interviews were filmed using a flip video camera and were translated and transcribed from at least three different languages. Several of the interviews were transcribed and translated but not all of them, owing to financial and time constraints. The video aspect is important because it captures both the poverty of the villages and the fact that this research was conducted at the height of the rainy season.

2 Melel Xojobal
Addressing the rights of child workers in Chiapas, Mexico

Introduction

Thousands of children live in precarious situations in the Mexican state of Chiapas, a community recovering from a deep-rooted violent conflict from 1994–2008 between the local indigenous communities, the Zapatistas and the military and police under the orders of the national government. Many families fled the rural areas to survive, and as migrants in the urban areas they have come to rely on their children, both boys and girls, to work on the streets seeking income in whatever way possible. These working children are especially numerous in San Cristóbal de la Casas, this is a popular tourist attraction where the children can raise money more easily than in quieter parts of the state of Chiapas. Some sell small legal items such as handicrafts, fruit and candies or provide small services such as running errands. Others sell drugs or their own bodies. This exploitation takes place within a context that fails to recognize the claims of children to be treated as subjects of rights, they need their families and communities to enable them to develop fully before asking them to cope with the responsibilities associated with adulthood. This study examines how Project Melel sought to enable the children to continue their education while at the same time bringing vital income to their families.

This chapter addresses both the potential and challenges of the rights-based education that Melel provides, and seeks to show how rights-based education can accomplish that which other approaches have failed to achieve, namely the fuller integration of these children into the body politic, improved educational achievements and access to redress for the structural and physical violence they undergo. In contrast to many other parts of Latin America where there has been a reduction in some of the child-work indicators and an increase in the number of children who attend school, the Chiapas indicators show no such improvement. The most vulnerable group to various forms of exploitation and abuse are migrant workers and families, and these constitute a particularly urgent target for research and revised public policy. As it is the children of migrant workers who are significantly more likely to work (and drop out of school), it is they who need the most immediate attention.

The children of Chiapas

Located on the border with Guatemala, and having a GDP of approximately $15 million, Chiapas is economically one of the poorest states in Mexico. A large indigenous population, primarily of Mayan descent, resides in the mountainous regions of central Chiapas. For the past two decades, beginning with the Zapatista rebellion of 1994, internal migration has characterized this region. Large groups of people of Tzotzil and Tseltal backgrounds have fled their highland communities (including Chamula, Huixtán, Chenahló, San Andrés Larraínzar, and Oxchuc) and have moved into the city of San Cristóbal de Las Casas. This migration has resulted in the loss of traditional patterns of protection associated with kin and community members, as well as by informal employers and patrons that families traditionally relied upon in their original rural areas. Moreover, the market-based social-policy reforms of the 1990s and early 2000s exacerbated the negative outcomes, especially on women, by, for example, reducing the already limited access that poorer families had to health care, pensions, schooling, and care for small children and the elderly. This situation is aggravated by the fact that many children can only speak their native tongue and thus feel intimidated by the thought of going to school, as Spanish is the official language in the schools of San Cristóbal. Thus teaching the children and their parents Spanish is a major goal of Melel.

Poverty, and in some cases violence, have followed all too many of these children of migrating families in their new communities. A few years ago approximately 2,700 children were reported to be working in the streets of San Cristóbal (Nečasová and Escalona 2010). Many of these child workers with whom Melel now works spend large parts of their day on the streets of downtown San Cristóbal where they engage in such activities as shining shoes, hawking wares, collecting garbage, and selling items in the market. They especially inhabit the well-known tourist areas that include the Cathedral Square in the town's center, the downtown market, the flea market, the People's Market of the South, and the Plaza de Santo Domingo. In most cases the children's income goes toward helping their families meet their basic needs: food, clothing, shelter, school and medical costs, transportation, and often the cost of raw material used in the family business. Despite income from the children the economic conditions of these families remains precarious.

Empirical data suggests that more boys than girls are involved in income-seeking child labor, both in Chiapas and globally. The work in which girls are engaged is often invisible because it occurs in the home. Labor for the girls means being left alone at home to care for their younger siblings or to carry out household chores while adults and older siblings are away at work or school. Such housework, which falls into the official category of "helping," never shows up in the statistics on the various members' contributions to family well-being. It is non-remunerative; only the act of earning one's own money is thus privileged. In San Cristóbal girls may be worse off for other reasons as well. Boys are less financially dependent upon adults. Not only does the average male street child earn about 200 pesos a week, he is often allowed to keep half of that wage, while handing the rest over to his mother to help her cover household expenses. Boys also have more freedom; they can pick up small jobs without reporting the income to their parents (Nečasová and Escalona 2010) As for the girls, because many of them work on the streets alongside their mothers, it is difficult to separate their earnings from their mothers'.

Physical violence and neglect form part of the everyday experience of these children. Violence in their lives takes many forms, notably being beaten within the family and exposed to violence in the street. Girls who remain at home to care for younger siblings, or who undertake household chores are vulnerable to aggression from neighbors and family members. The boys are less likely to suffer from violence at home because they operate within a social context of informal street communities as street vendors, trash collectors, or shoe-shiners. They may, however, also be victimized by neighbors, family members, and people they meet on the street. Although hard data is difficult to come by, many children in Chiapas have experienced domestic violence.

A groundbreaking 2010 UN report on violence notes that some groups of children including migrant children and child workers, and those from ethnic minorities and other marginalized groups are particularly vulnerable to violence.[1] This report also points out that the silence about the abuses children suffer is most notable within such marginalized groups. Silence and the lack of reporting and hard data make the educators' work more difficult, as they seek to curtail the violence that threatens children in the communities in which they work.

Children in these migrant communities also experience parental neglect. This is often difficult to identify and even harder to prevent, given the acute poverty in which their families live. Neglect means that parents or caregivers fail to address, let alone meet a child's physical and emotional needs, even when they have the means, knowledge, and access to services to do so. They also frequently fail to keep their children out of danger. This pattern of neglect extends to a failure to utilize child health and welfare services, or to provide children with documentation, such as the birth certificates they need to participate in services. Given the context of poverty, within which such failures occur, it is by no means easy to distinguish between those that are caused deliberately and those that result from either ignorance or lack of concern on the part of parents and public officials.

The origin of Melel's Human Rights Education Project

Over the past decade a number of organizations in Chiapas have adopted a rights-based approach to developing programs for children. This reflects a shift away from a welfare model and includes not only rights-based empowerment but also attention to gender differences. The old charity-model failed children because it did little to bring these most vulnerable populations into the social and political life of the nation. Further, because it had no built-in acknowledgement of gender discrimination, the particular concerns of girls went unaddressed.

In the mid 1990s, around the time of the Zapatista uprising, churches and other development organizations began to adopt the new rights-based approaches where the goal was to empower ordinary citizens to engage in the political struggle. Churches, particularly those within the Archdiocese of Chiapas under the leadership of Bishop Samuel Ruiz García, began to impart a human rights message and to mobilize communities to fight for their rights. This transition in the 1990s resulted in many church groups converting themselves into agents of civil society. In contrast with the old charity approach, a rights-based approach focuses on the structural causes that foster such social ills and human rights abuses as discrimination, the lack of access to education and social protection, while emphasizing the importance of income-generating modalities. This approach relies heavily upon community organization and education as the best ways to empower the people politically, and to improve the living conditions of the poor. Today these organizations continue to struggle to find the best balance between meeting children's needs whilst instilling in the children and their families a sense of rights-based advocacy.

Melel Xojobal, (which in Tzotzil means "true light" or "shine a light"), was founded by Dominican friars in 1997 as a non-governmental organization in the city of San Cristóbal de Las Casas. As mentioned earlier, at first Melel modeled itself on the charity approach to assistance, in keeping with its religious traditions. However, as Melel's director Patricia Figueroa has observed, this approach of giving away goods and services to the poor caused families to rely too much on Melel in helping them to meet their basic needs. In order to move beyond this approach and emulate the rights-based approaches now being adopted by children's organizations elsewhere in the world, in 2006 Melel joined the Child Right's Network in Mexico, an umbrella group of organizations working with children. Becoming part of this network strengthened Melel's resolve to restructure the way the organization provides for needy families by providing assistance within a human rights framework.

Melel has struggled on behalf of its children in a quest to bring them better opportunities and greater security. Melel is primarily an organization created to uphold the rights of child workers, and thus the problems associated with child labor are a central concern. As policy, Melel opposes the prohibition of child work; it does not support legislation that seeks to prohibit children from working. Melel views the work of girls and boys as being an unavoidable consequence of poverty, and believes that this poverty must be addressed first. Thus, for example, instead of criminalizing child-work, it seeks to help girls and boys achieve better working conditions in decent environments where they are treated fairly, with such improvements serving as a springboard to a full awareness of their rights. Melel takes the stance that governments and other social agencies must support a child's right to work. If children are forced to give up their work because it is prohibited by law, and if no government or other support is provided for them, then the lives of such working children are likely to become worse.

It is worth taking a moment to look at this statement from Melel's website, which has been posted in response to a Mexican law seeking to provide holistic protection of the rights of the child:

To make laws that don't guarantee the fulfillment of the rights of boys and girls and to promote the eradication of child work without taking into consideration the structural causes denotes a deep lack of recognition of the reality endured by millions of girl and boy workers, negates their condition as active social subjects, and leaves them in a state of complete vulnerability. We recognize all the thousands of young workers of Chiapas, and call upon the government to put aside the dependency approach and promote the respect, defense, and fulfillment of the human rights of children and youth.[2]

Those on the other side of the debate believe that the elimination of child labor is a prerequisite for the realization of children's right to an education. They note the evidence that indicates that when child workers attend school, they tend to achieve lower learning outcomes than do children who are not working. Such findings have been one of the factors behind the introduction of a range of legislative reforms seeking to begin to end child labor. Legislation in many countries is not consistent with the International Labor Organization (ILO) Convention 138, Article 2, establishing the minimum age for full-time work (14 in developing countries) and that for leaving school (15). In the absence of national legislation in Mexico ensuring such standards, children can legitimately be employed at an age when they should be getting a full-time education. The introduction of a minimum wage, applicable equally to children, is designed to discourage employers from using children as a source of cheap labor. The ILO also calls for legislation that prohibits the use of children in hazardous, harmful, and exploitative forms of work, and to bring domestic legislation into line with the standards defined in Article 32 of the Convention on the Rights of the Child.

As part of its rights-based approach to street workers and street children Melel works with parents, teachers and communities in order to effect change and to bring working children and their families into the political process. As a kind of corollary, Melel argues that government should not seek to eliminate child work altogether, but rather make itself more accountable to the children's needs.

Melel's educational approach

A major obstacle facing Melel in this work within the larger Mexican culture is that children are not seen as rights-holders. Thus one of their central tasks was to help the rest of the society to see children, and especially child workers, as having rights that must be respected. Melel struggled because it works with a population that often has little or no knowledge of rights, including its existing rights in both Mexican, and international human rights laws, statutes and practices. Thus the dual goal of Melel's educational work has been to empower children and to raise their and their parents' awareness of human rights. Melel works on the assumption that the needs of children can only be met to a sustainable degree when the children and their families know the children's rights to basic public services, and that the government is legally obligated to provide them. Melel also recognizes another major obstacle, namely that of the long-standing discrimination against the Mayan community and especially towards those who had migrated to the cities. This discrimination resulted in the children both being treated badly, if not violently, and their exclusion from access to the basic education system.

Melel identified five major human rights issues that the Mayan children faced in their lives at home and on the street seeking money to support themselves and perhaps also their families: (1) the dangers and conditions they encountered in their daily work; (2) the lack of access to an education; (3) the presence of physical violence; (4) the lack of official identity papers; and (5) the suppressed freedom of information and expression. All of these issues and rights are interrelated; all are in some way related to the discrimination faced by the Mayan group as a whole. The children are, however, both the most vulnerable and the most likely victims. Melel's human rights education program addresses each of these issues.

The Melel website describes some of their educational activities as follows:

> Workshops were held with parents and community members on various topics including: Your Right to Health Care, Healthy Development in Early Childhood, How to Monitor Your Child's Height and Weight, How to Provide a Healthy Diet for Your Child, and Prevention of Childhood Illnesses. The children were monitored as to their height and weight with special attention being given to those children who were underweight. While the children are eating properly, only 70 percent have reached their expected height and weight. Home visits were also conducted to help understand each child's circumstances. Abuse and mistreatment were also addressed in workshops. These workshops focused on violence in the family and preventing child sex abuse. The workshops were well attended and participants learned to exercise their rights to a life free of violence and how to recognize the symptoms of child abuse and to whom to report incidences of child abuse.

The same website reports:

> A total of 27 boys and girls between the ages of several months and four years participated in educational activities to promote their cognitive, emotional, socio-affective skills, and to ensure their healthy physical development. A cooked breakfast and lunch was served every day during the week and any health problems they had were dealt with. These children also received a pre-school education and professional support to ensure their healthy development. Talks were held with parents on enrollment procedures for pre-school. They were also instructed in how to obtain birth certificates and the necessity of registering their children for school.

Melel's website's English language page states:

> Bilingualism is central to Melel Xojobal's mission. Staff are evenly divided between Mayas and mestizos, and all Spanish speakers must learn an indigenous language. Melel has turned this need into a unique opportunity: they ask the children to teach staff their languages. By reversing the power dynamic and placing the indigenous child in the position of "he who is supposed to know," they have found a tremendous surge in pride and ability among the youth. This technique has also helped to overcome one of Melel's persistent problems: children's rejection of compassion (afecto). Because of cultural reasons and alienation, many children reject affection; teaching their language provides another path for connection.[3]

Melel organizes Learning Circles in which the educators utilize a pedagogy which is typical in non-formal education settings. Often "classes" are held on the streets or in the markets near where the children work. The educators have been prepared to select from a range of potential learning situations where the children can actively engage in critical thinking as the educators, in their role as facilitators, guide the process and contribute informed input, where and when necessary. Typically, the Learning Circles begin with the children being allowed to say what they already know, whether right or wrong, about the topic under discussion. This is followed by the presentation of practical exercises through which they can discover and learn new ideas, correct misconceptions and gain new insights. In practice the learners and the facilitators learn from each other. Most importantly, the children become active subjects of their learning as opposed to just passive receivers of knowledge, thus preparing them to become active in other decisions that impact their lives (Freire 1970).

While Melel's educational approach has yet to be thoroughly evaluated, it has developed its own unique methodology that introduces children to human rights, one that incorporates the indigenous history and culture of the children and their families. For example, they introduce the children to ideas about human rights by discussing the Tzotzil expression, Lekil Kuxlejal, which means "a good life." The broader concept which Melel promotes is that Lekil Kuxlejal comprises a set of ecological and moral conditions based on the integration between society and nature. The happiness of the community is linked with the environment and ecosystem. In the eyes of another Mayan group, Tzeltal, all humans possess the same rights. Ultimately, however, it is the community members themselves who must decide what steps must be taken to achieve "the good life." These and other cultural concepts which define rules for social relations are used by educators to show that children have rights and that parents and the government ought to respect those rights (Nečasová and Escalona 2010).

Efficacy as the heart of Melel's Human Rights Education Program

Efficacy is at the heart of Melel's approach to children's rights education. This concept has two chief components: the ability to control one's life, and the power to effect change by one's actions. Whether the efficacy or empowerment is low or high, the concept is closely connected to human motivation, well-being, and accomplishment. People with low efficacy are those who give up easily and are convinced of the futility of their efforts. Efficacy is taught in order to increase peoples' feelings of well-being and personal security (Bandura 1997). This analysis is especially pertinent to the case of girls and women who suffer depression and loneliness. These two problems associated with personal well-being are seen to be especially prevalent within the migrant Mayan families served by Melel (Nečasová and Escalona 2010). Educating for increased efficacy is a pressing need for communities where there are high levels of structural discrimination and violence.

Melel's needs assessment recognizes that children and their families exist within larger social systems, and that such systems must be addressed if children's rights are to be respected. In other words, efficacy is a society-wide problem and therefore must be strengthened throughout. Melel's goals include having children and their families reflect on and change children's roles and responsibilities. It also recognizes that the ideas, attitudes, values and skills that underpin efficacy must be instilled early in life in order to influence the political system and the responsiveness, style, accountability, and trustworthiness of government institutions and officials. Melel's strategy is to improve efficacy at three levels—(a) individual or personal; (b) proxy, namely those persons with whom the children interact on a daily basis (notably parents and teachers); and (c) the collective—that is, those individuals and institutions that define the social environment in which the children live. Action at all these levels is seen as necessary to ensure the protection and the empowerment of the children.

With respect to personal efficacy, exercised individually, each individual needs to bring his or her influence on their own ways of living and their responses to their immediate political and social environment. Melel uses Learning Circles or weekly discussion groups held either on the streets or at its headquarters to engage children in reflective exercises that help them to determine what they might wish to change about their daily lives. Through these discussions children learn not just about their rights as workers, but also ethical concepts such as that boys and girls have equal rights and that to hit someone is a form of abuse. They are encouraged to share what they have learned with their parents and their friends.

A teacher at Melel has reported how the children, as a result of their participation in Melel's Learning Circles, grow both in confidence and in their ability to make difficult, life-altering decisions. In one notable case a child came to Melel asking to be separated from his family and admitted to a shelter. While the cause of this request was heart-breaking—he was being beaten at home—once empowered, this youth took it upon himself to get out of an abusive situation. According to Patricia Figueroa, one of the measures of success in Melel's human rights education occurs when children approach her to share tales of domestic violence, and to seek support from her and other Melel staff (Nečasová and Escalona 2010: 19). Recognition of a rights-violation is an important first step. Even more heartening is the growth in personal efficacy—belief in oneself and one's ability to effect change. This is revealed when people begin to speak about the violations.

Unfortunately the children who do seek help are not the norm. Most children have little direct control over the social conditions, institutions and practices that affect their everyday lives. The appeals and instruction in personal efficacy can only go so far. Children must turn to parents or to teachers for help in standing up for their rights. This is why Melel also works with "proxies" to improve efficacy, with the first such proxy always being a parent. Melel's work with parents has numerous interesting aspects.

First, Melel educators recognize that the parents (Melel prioritizes mothers, in terms of the participants in its educational programming) may also have experienced feelings of low efficacy themselves. Melel conducts workshops for them to address the issues they face, notably domestic violence, sexual abuse, and child labor. The basic supposition is that parents and teachers who are confident in their ability to make change happen will model that behavior for the children. Further, self-efficacious or empowered parents become strong advocates for their children in their interactions with social institutions (Bandura 1997). Melel therefore seeks to improve the behavior-management skills of parents and caregivers by encouraging them to see the value of sending their children to school and of learning about, and respecting their children's rights.

It is not enough, however, to present parents with information and then leave them to take action. Melel recognizes that a long-lasting relationship with parents is essential. Only when trust has been built up between the parents and the educators do parents feel comfortable sharing with them concerns about their children. Melel is especially proud of its success in building a trusting relationship with parents. One welcome result has been to persuade them to reduce the number of hours their children work so that they can spend more time on their school-work (Nečasová and Escalona 2010: 19).

Parents cannot be the only proxies seeking to protect children and safeguard their rights, they cannot always effectively protect the rights of their own children. Thus Melel's rights' approach also mobilizes educators and other school staff members to remind parents that children have a right to attend school; that their parents must send them to school, and that children's education must come before their work. When parents do not comply, Melel educators step in as advocates for children, especially when children are too fearful to approach a parent or a teacher. A similar situation is illuminated by the words of a child in Mérida:

> I knew that my mother didn't want me to work. She wanted me to do well enough in school to pass the sixth grade, so I could find a job in a local

factory. But she had to take me along to Mérida, because she needed me to sell from one tray of roses while she sold from the other. One day I made the decision to tell her that I didn't want to go with her. I told her that I was ashamed of selling, and that I didn't like the other people in the place where we worked. She got really angry.

To keep parents from making choices that may not be in the best interests of their children, Melel makes it mandatory for the children to attend school regularly if they want to remain part of Melel. Most children attend primary or lower secondary school. For those who already have left school before the eighth grade, Melel tries to get them back into schools and encourages them to complete their primary schooling. The positive impact of working with parents to ensure children's rights is illustrated by this anecdote reported by a researcher. A woman, the mother of four daughters, was expelled from the town of San Juan Chamula on religious grounds, and moved to San Cristóbal. None of her daughters had a birth certificate. The educators explained to the mother why it was important to obtain a birth certificate for her daughters, and how demanding this right would help her children in other ways beyond just access to education. The mother finally obtained the birth certificates and now her daughters attend school; one was even given a scholarship on the strength of her academic performance. This woman, who is adamant about improving her family's economic situation, is now an active participant in Melel—as is evidenced by her regular attendance at the parent meetings organized by Melel (Nečasová and Escalona 2010: 37).

Because school is so central to the fulfillment of a child's human rights, school officials and teachers are important proxies for working children. The intensity of a teacher's belief in her instructional efficacy will partly determine how she structures academic activities in the classroom. This in turn inevitably impacts students' academic development and their judgments of their intellectual capabilities. Teachers with high self-efficacy create rewarding experiences for their students (Bandura 1997). Melel works on an individual basis with local public-school officials to ensure that the schools accept and retain the students and support their academic achievement. Melel also works with individual teachers to help them understand the special needs of working children, needs which are different from those of children who do not have to work to help support their family. In addition to meeting their needs, the teachers are encouraged to value any special strengths unique to working children.

Melel's use of efficacy-driven children's rights education works to upgrade children's sense of personal efficacy and that of the parents and teachers as proxy efficacy-boosters. The third component of Melel's strategy is to support children's ability to effect change through collective efficacy. The various children's rights agencies in San Cristóbal are encouraged to pool their knowledge, skills, and resources, so as to provide mutual support, form alliances, and work together to secure what they cannot accomplish on their own. Melel believes that a community's shared belief in its joint capability to bring desired changes into people's lives is the root of collective agency. The process tends to be self-strengthening. The experience of collective efficacy intensifies the community's vision of what they are able to achieve, enhancing their motivational commitment and strengthening their resilience to adversity (ibid.). Many children and their families who are part of the Melel organization develop an identity of "student-worker" and are thereby empowered to resist external subjugation through bonding with their fellow student workers.

Melel is not the only place where children have reported learning that they have rights. Schools and homes are also mentioned. The difference is that the latter fail to link having rights with the pursuit of efficacy or the empowerment of the students, their parents, their teachers and the other community actors. In its pursuit of heightened efficacy, Melel imparts the skills children need to participate socially and to have their views heard. At Melel both the children and their family members are encouraged to express their views, to seek information, and to have their opinions count. Melel bases all this work in the participation rights enunciated in articles 12 and 13 of the UN Convention on the Rights of the Child.

Assessment of learning and the challenges ahead

> When asked about what children in Chiapas are missing, the answers were very revealing about the specific situation of this group of children, as their responses were generally closely linked with their family lives. The most important rights to them are having a bath, having a house made of concrete, having a safe door, having a whole family and having respect and love and tenderness.
>
> (Nečasová and Escalona 2010: 39)

The impact of Melel's work was measured by the researcher who used interviews and drawings by 36 children (10–14 years old) to assess their knowledge of rights. Generally speaking, the analysis shows that the majority, and especially the older children, had a concept of their having rights or claims on society. The specific rights they identified were closely associated with their daily lives and aspirations. Their drawings described how they would like to see their lives, their houses, their families, the games they would like to play and their conditions of daily life. Their drawings and interviews also tell much about the difficulties that arise in their daily life, notably access to education, freedom from street and domestic violence, conditions of poverty and marginalization, and abandonment by one or both parents. The differences between the boys and girls was notable with respect to levels of neglect and violence, and especially because the girls, whether also working on the street or not, were also expected to perform household tasks. The rights the boys and girls valued most were to family, to play, to go to school, to have clothes, and to have respect and love. Older students also identified work as a right.

Further research would be necessary to assess the impact of this knowledge on their families, the later lives of the children, and on the community as a whole. This understanding should not be attributed only to the work of Melel, but also to the children's learning in school. Most of the rights the children knew about and deemed important were those that pertained to home, namely physical security and family life. They made no mention of political or civil rights, of discrimination and political instability, and they certainly never spoke about the government's responsibility to safeguard their rights to political participation within their communities. Their emphasis on family ties in with Melel's goal to strengthen the children's rights at home. Physical insecurity was a prominent theme in their drawings. The children talked about experiencing the consequences of structural and physical violence in almost all domains of their lives. And yet the absence of recognition of other rights or government responsibility or the structural causes underlying rights violations alarmed some of the Melel educators.

Conclusion

Inspiring as Melel's approach is, the fact remains that many of its children still struggle to stay in school, and many of their needs remain unaddressed. It is clear that the range of their choices, and thus their personal efficacy, is constrained by overwhelming obstacles linked to poverty, discrimination, social marginalization, and violence. While cultural factors account for some of the gender disparities and the violence faced by these children, it is a lack of opportunity more than anything else that is at the root of their rights violations. This is further aggravated by the fact that public opinion does not support the rights of indigenous children, or the integration of their families into Mexico's economic and political mainstream. Working children and their families still must endure the centuries of discrimination and stereotyping imposed upon them by society. Public opinion blames parents for their supposed "failure" to keep their children off the streets, and opinion also is shaped by the fact that children who work are seen as violating the almost sacred norm of childhood. The prevalence of such a social view enables the governments to avoid having to provide the specific protections the children need. Thus a major challenge faced by Melel and other children's aid organizations in Chiapas is to encourage the Mexican government and its citizenry as a whole to see indigenous children as rights holders. Their first and continuing challenge, however, is to convince the children themselves that they have rights. Many educators feel that they are still falling short, and that it is contingent upon them to improve their programming.

Notes

1 www.unicef.org/protection/CP_Thematic_Report_2010(1).pdf.
2 Available at melelxojobal.org.mx.
3 Available at www.shinealight.org/Melel.html.

3 Education to address violence against women in rural Peru

Introduction: Institute for Legal Defense's history of human rights education

The Institute for Legal Defense (IDL), the primary educational agency in this study, is a Lima-based NGO committed to HRE in economically and politically marginalized communities in Cusco, Peru. IDL identifies the causes of poverty prevalent in rural areas, as the poor social and economic conditions in which the communities live, and illiteracy, which is aggravated by indifference and incompetence on the part of state officials. The conditions of the women and their children are, according to IDL, further exacerbated by the traditional, male-defined, social roles in their communities and by the women's lack of awareness of their civil and human rights and of the mechanisms through which they may obtain redress and compliance. IDL therefore chose to work with women in these marginalized communities who were suffering systemic human rights abuses and lacked effective access to legal recourse through the state's judicial apparatus.

One of IDL's objectives has been to improve the quality of citizen participation in public debates and in the development of state reform processes. Inspired by the experience of popular education associated with Paulo Freire, its educational aims are to create a political consciousness for social transformation and to generate new attitudes (or strengthen those already existing), which can serve as the basis for the consolidation of democratic values and an environment that is respectful of human rights. IDL therefore works to develop active citizenship skills and practices on the part of the vulnerable groups with whom they work, and to increase the awareness and responsiveness of state and municipal authorities with respect to the problems and demands of the communities they serve (Benoît and Verona Badajoz 2010).

To show support for local communities and later to address the needs of rural and indigenous women and children, Community Defenders (CDs) were created in 1992 by the Peruvian government and have since also enjoyed the sustained support of UNICEF. Today this structure enables women, especially those in local communities, to organize and seek aid from the government. Until the arrival of IDL the local groups of Community Defenders around Cusco were focused on meeting the rights and needs of women, as mothers responsible for the health and welfare of their families, through access to government social services. When IDL arrived in 2003 with a grant from the government, they persuaded the Community Defender groups around Cusco to expand their agenda to focus on their rights, and especially those rights associated with freedom from violence.[1] Fulfilling this broader role of the Community Defenders required empowering communities through a process of collective citizenship, that is by enabling the Defenders who were mostly women to participate in community decision-making, especially in those decisions that lead to better access to justice for women and children who were the victims of violence. The new objectives were determined by IDL in 2005 through a process of discussions with the government, UNICEF and local communities.[2]

In addition to establishing these objectives and thereby reorienting the Community Defenders' work, IDL has supported the efforts of the CDs to bring cases of violence against women and children to local courts in the communities where they work. Reporting the cases is designed to teach other women who are victims of violence or discrimination, how they and their children can gain access to justice, as well as to health services and education, and thus fully exercise and benefit from their citizenship. Capacity-building was provided by IDL to enable CDs to increase and evaluate rights-awareness and rights-advocacy within the various communities in which the CDs operated. Continuing human rights education is seen by IDL as a strategy to develop effective citizenship and active political consciousness on the part of the CDs and the vulnerable and marginalized groups they work with.

IDL identifies four overall goals of HRE to be implemented through the work of the CDs in the local communities: (1) to create a political consciousness for social transformation; (2) to generate new (or strengthen existing) attitudes needed to consolidate democratic values and an environment respectful of human rights; (3) develop active citizens among the vulnerable groups with which it works; and (4) enhance awareness among authorities (municipal or state) with respect to the problems and demands of the population. As emphasized in the fourth goal, IDL believes that democratization prospers when it is supported by human rights education programs, not only for ordinary citizens, but also for the relevant local and state officials. This education for the officials emphasizes how they must recognize and develop a rights-based understanding of the issues they deal with and how the issues are shaped by local culture and gender bias.

In addition to its work in Cusco the IDL-CD project works in these other departments: Ayacucho, Junín, and Huancavelica. In all of these places where the conflict during the 1980s and into the 1990s hit hardest, the IDL's HRE work has been strongly influenced by the need to prevent more experiences like those of the civil war and the political violence, during which the rights of the rural populations were systematically violated. IDL-CD provides training in human rights to target populations composed of women's groups, local officials, and authorities. Before describing in more detail what this training entails we turn to discussion of the problem that IDL is seeking to address through HRE.

Cusco: violence against women and limited access to justice in rural areas

The IDL-Community Defender Project is based in six rural communities in the Cusco region (Canas, Chumbivilcas, Cusco, Espinar, Paruro, and Paucartambo) comprising 53 percent of the total population of the department. Largely a Quecha speaking indigenous population, during the twenty years of fighting between the Sendero Luminoso and the national military the communities suffered massive dislocation and violence. Moreover most members of these communities do not speak Spanish, making it hard for them to access government services. Except for Cusco itself, the population is completely rural and lives in communities that have extremely limited access to state services, including those related to the justice system. One of the most significant handicaps faced by the rural communities, and women in particular, is illiteracy. Among the consequences of these and other cultural conditions is that few women hold places of public responsibility, or are in a position to improve the situation of women as a whole.

Although the data are still limited, the extent of violence against women in the Cusco region is particularly alarming. The major response of the state so far has been to pass the Law on Protection Against Family Violence[3] and to create intervention programs. Unfortunately, the law is based on an urban, centralist vision of the problem as opposed to one adapted to rural conditions, where government services are absent and distant from the women's daily lives (Benoît and Verona Badajoz 2010). As a result most rural women do not seek help as often as their urban counterparts. The results from a World Health Organization study show that only one in four women who had been victims of violence actually sought institutional support by going to police stations or the courts.[4] The minimal presence of the state justice system has led victims of violence to believe that they cannot expect a response or formal redress.

On the other side of the equation is the justice system from which these women facing violence should be able to seek redress. The presence of the state and the quality of its services is very limited in rural areas in Peru. The Peruvian judicial system, for example, provides one judge for every 17,628 inhabitants. The state's judicial services are concentrated in the provincial capitals. Thus, rural communities have limited access to the formal justice system. Corruption, giant caseloads and backlogs in the courts have led to one of the highest national rates of citizen disapproval, with 78 percent of the Peruvian population expressing dissatisfaction with the judicial system. Two of the Community Defenders interviewed for this project shared these perceptions:

> When there is a question of criminal violence, the law states that there must be a punishment for a convicted offender. It also points out what the punishment should be: community service. But in reality this is not the practice; until now we do not know of any aggressor who has served his community service as punishment for the aggression he has inflicted on his family.
>
> (Toribio, Community Defender, Interview with Verona Badajoz, Cusco, May 2010)

Another factor which undermines the law is corruption [...] starting with our police and ending with the judiciary. This is another important factor. Therefore, the state should put this in order by making sure the law is enforced, punishing people who are bribed, that are bought off, whether they are authorities, police or the judiciary.
(Manuela, Community Defender, Interview with Verona Badajoz, Cusco, May 2010)

Other practices and obstacles that diminish the quality of services that ought to protect the rights of the rural population are deeply rooted forms of discrimination—ethnic or otherwise. They include lack of access to basic state and community services, disregard for privacy and confidentiality, and the lack of specialized skills on the issue of violence. Two Community Defenders described their perception of the capabilities of state judicial officers as follows:

Why is there no compliance with the law? Because of the ignorance and negligence of the authorities! Perhaps the fact that they are unaware of their duties also makes them unaware of the law.
(Libertad, Community Defender, Interview with Verona Badajoz, Cusco, May 2010)

The prosecutors or judges, who handle the law, should know more about their roles and what rules actually fulfill our Constitution, that's the law. Perhaps these gentlemen officials are not updated, do not revise their manuals, they are not aware of the Constitution. Then do not apply the laws as they should be. What you should do is enforce the laws.
(Justina, Community Defender, Interview with Verona Badajoz, Cusco, May 2010)

Within the department of Cusco, the institutional actors to be found in the rural communities include peasant patrols, the community councils, the Community Defenders and Justices of the Peace. The latter are the sole representatives of formal State justice. Justices of the Peace and community leaders often prevent social conflicts from becoming violent, and the solutions that result may often be more effective than the established legal norms. Their way of administering justice is faster, more effective and less expensive. They also retain high levels of legitimacy within the population, in a manner notably distinct from that achieved by the state institutions.

The officials within the State justice system (such as the judiciary and the National Ministry of Justice) are located exclusively in the provincial capitals, and, as mentioned above, do not reach the majority of the rural population. In contrast, police stations cover a larger area, with establishments in many districts. However, with respect to the particular needs of women's access to justice, the police generally do not have the competence or training needed to meet these or other judicial demands emanating from the communities in which they are situated. Victims of violence who want to channel their complaints must use the current judicial system (formal and centralized), an arduous and expensive process that is difficult to access (Benoît and Verona Badajoz 2010).

IDL's work with the Community Defenders, which we turn to in the next section, has addressed the violence against women in rural areas, especially within the family. This reflects both the increased levels of violence in communities all over Latin America and the degree to which the violence is exacerbated by state policies that ignore the peculiar circumstances and conditions of rural and multicultural communities as described above. However IDL believes that in addition to promoting access to justice for women victims of violence in rural areas, their work must also address domestic violence in particular. A culture of peace within the whole community depends on its primary social unit, the family. The Peruvian family structure and behaviors are deeply rooted in the culture of machismo. This complex of attitudes has become a widespread ideology nurtured over generations. This permits male practitioners to rationalize domestic violence as normal, justified, and indeed as the duty of husbands towards both their wives and their children. The violence is generally borne by the female victims as an established cultural norm (Benoît and Verona Badajoz 2010). One Community Defender points out:

> Men easily convince the court; many judges believe men more than the women. Indeed, for women there is no justice. Sometimes the judge or prosecutor would say, "You are to blame, as a woman should serve."
> (Mary, Community Defender, Interview with Verona Badajoz, Cusco, May 2010)

Unemployment and its associated frustrations aggravate the conditions that result in male violence against women and children. Complaints by women or external actors often generate the opposite effect of that which was intended; namely, the men feel that they may lose their authority and thus augment the violence against their woman and children. This cycle reinforces the women's self-image of vulnerability, defining themselves as victims in need of male "protection." They find it difficult to grasp the idea that they possess rights and freedoms, and that there is a legal system out there able to protect them.

The IDL community defenders and the human rights education training

In several communities people have created alternative community-based systems to administer justice and resolve disputes. These community justice mechanisms have evolved and now even share offices with those of the official administration of justice. Some rural communities have created autonomous formal systems of justice—communal police, peasant patrols, and the Community Defenders—with replacing institutions like Justices of the Peace, which then constitute a sort of middle ground between the legal systems. IDL has found that once women have access to leadership positions, they are able to generate important changes in laws and practices, most notably incorporating sanctions against domestic violence and the recognition of equal status for all women. All of this has boosted the ability of the justice system and local leaders to upgrade the status of women in these rural villages.

IDL considers the Community Defenders as key in the strategy for access to justice for rural women affected by violence. Human rights education and training are designed for the CDs in order to build their capacity and empower them. The strategy is based on a social analysis that emphasizes three concepts: justice, gender, and power. Defenders are taught through human rights education programs about international human rights and the legitimacy of demands for access to and participation in the process of justice. They also are taught the knowledge and skills needed for active citizenship, both individually and collectively.

IDL sees human rights education as a process that should be continually reinforced. This is achieved, for instance, through the study of the legal tools in order to expand the women's knowledge of the enforceability of rights, the development of empowerment strategies for the exercise of rights, and awareness training for civil servants with respect to different rights. In training sessions IDL places a strong emphasis on generating awareness among citizens of their being both active agents, and subjects of rights. Training also emphasizes empowerment skills and the importance of reflection on one's own situation and environment. These were important learning objectives in the first stage of the project. From this education local initiatives emerged, coupled with a change of attitude towards human rights and the need to bring about social change.

This package of knowledge, skills, and attitudes provided crucial skills for the formation of the Defenders. The process, however, was less about teaching skills and focused more on specific problems associated with the women's experience of violence and their need to obtain access to justice. By analyzing the concrete situation, the women identified the skills and knowledge they needed to seek redress. This analysis was based on the women sharing their real-life experiences and how they dealt with them, especially when they tried to change the situation within their families. The task of the group of facilitators was to respond to the demands and needs of women as they were formulated on the basis of their group discussions. Moreover, the facilitators were women who themselves had progressed through the system from being victims, to being able to facilitate redress through their own actions. The sessions were thus discussions about the women's personal experiences and social analyses of causes and potential remedies, especially though access to the court system.

An important part of the process of group critical thinking is the analysis of situations by examining the underlying reasons, ideas, behavior and available information. The sessions encouraged frank debates with special attention to the cultural and social obstacles that women face in obtaining redress. In the process the main task of the discussion leaders or facilitators was to enable the women to address the issues systematically, one by one, distinguishing between problems, social circumstances, and remedies. IDL prepared cases and problems for the women to debate. They also outlined the skills, attitudes and information they expected the women to develop during the course of each session. The basic sequence model is that of see, judge, and act. To promote their analytical skills the women were often encouraged to develop symbolic representations of the problem. One such symbol was the tree, breaking the image down to its original seed, its growth, its leaves, and its cultivation. This image was favored because it was a positive way to illustrate the need for, the role of, and the various stages of capacity building. The leaders also encouraged the women to think of themselves as leaders and thus as needing to acquire the appropriate skills, central to which were those associated with decision-making, communication, and team work. IDL developed detailed protocols in order to enable the facilitators to plan and then analyze the evolution of a session through written reports on each of their workshops. IDL has also developed syllabi that set out learning at different levels, defined as basic training, social leadership, legal leadership and educational and political leadership. Each level has its own goals and curriculum. However, all are designed to be closely linked to the problems faced by the workshop participants in their daily lives and the action they can take to address them.

Human rights educators have a long way to go. The analysis of the interviews conducted on IDL's work reveals that local judicial officials commonly acknowledge that men and women have equal rights. They claim that women also know their rights, and that those rights are now being respected. However, the analysis of concrete situations shows that the reality does not always reflect the theory. At the community level, there is a strong contrast between responses from women and those from men, especially in relation to situations that differentially affect men and women:

> When the men allow it, women participate in the assembly, but more often they are not allowed to participate; women do not express their views to the community as a whole. They remain silent and accept decisions without protesting. The municipal authorities have agreed that women should participate when the tasks of women are in question and when times get tough. When they are pregnant, we cannot make them work so much. Sometimes they are made to carry so much that would not be good for anyone.
> (Manuela, Community Defender, Interview with Verona Badajoz, Cusco, May 2010)

Some men say that, in principle, women have the same rights as men and therefore should not be abused. In practice, however, women often remain silent and do not report abusive treatment, even shifting the responsibility for the abuse towards themselves as victims. In this regard, a male villager said, "Now the women do not know how to behave towards their spouses (…). For this reason a man beats his wife." He then noted that the solution to the problem of violence is to inform the community of their rights, and to treat men and women as equals. Members of the Community Defenders within these same communities adopt a different approach. They are more vocal about explicitly recognizing and addressing the sexism present in their communities. As a premise for discussing abuse, they refer to machismo and to male-control mechanisms such as the handling of family money and income. Human rights educators know that they must address these mechanisms of control that are especially central in situations where the women neither work for pay nor have ability to do so, thus contributing to their systematic exclusion from decision-making and access to independence.

The impact of the IDL-CD's human rights education approach

IDL now believes that the primary goal of the Community Defenders has been largely accomplished. It has set in motion systems, knowledge and practices that will in the long run help the women to obtain greater and better access to justice. It has upgraded a stable state-supported institution, the CDs. Individual officers and ordinary citizens are now seen to have learned to respond positively to problems, injustices and violations of human rights through the judicial process. IDL is optimistic about sustainability due to the creation of a sub-program entitled "Access to Justice" specifically to address the problem of violence against indigenous and peasant women. Its goal is to promote the consolidation of, and cooperation among the relevant regional actors, the empowerment of local women leaders in this field and the mobilization of community actors (like the Justices of the Peace and other representatives of the judiciary). IDL created Access to Justice to sustain the learning and build upon what has been learned to channel future educational activities. Unfortunately this new entity still depends on external funds, and these have not been forthcoming.[5]

Time will tell as to whether all the elements needed for sustainability have been established. The most basic component, the consciousness among the women that they and their children have rights, and that the courts are required to, and can bring them redress, is now part of the public consciousness in the region. An equally important accomplishment of the Defenders during the last ten years was the consolidation of the institutional structure of both the Defenders and its regional integration through the Departmental Coordinator of Community Defenders of Cusco (CODECC). This shift enabled the two groups to become effective in strategic partnerships in their work in the larger Cusco region. Members of these groups also became human rights educators in their own communities, addressing a wider agenda of justice concerns beyond domestic violence and gender sensitivity.

The Defenders have become important resources in these communities for the protection of rights and in gaining access to justice. Successful social change in one area changed the general mentality and opened up the possibility for other changes. Most notable were new experiences of participation and advocacy at the local government level, and even at the level of regional government. The advocacy- and capacity-building work of the Defenders and the CODECC has illustrated how institutions of civil society can have a positive effect on the perception communities have of themselves and of their capacities. The Defenders now craft their own agenda on the basis of the expressed needs and demands of the population. IDL helped to strengthen the regional economic base of the Defenders and the CODECC, and to promote coordination with the municipal authorities and the state judicial officials. The benefits of this educational outreach strategy reach all members of the communities in which they work. They see how women's access to gender equality and justice in their social and political lives benefits the whole community.

Crucial to success is the strategy to develop the networking capability of the Community Defenders of Cusco, to enable them to work with a range of local institutions and community groups in order to build the synergies necessary to optimize local conflict resolution and the observance of human rights. These groups include justices, peasant patrols, peasant communities, women's organizations and Community Defenders. The IDL team sought to empower these various actors through advising and training in skills that promote human rights and reduce community violence and discrimination against women.

The education of both the officials and the women, coupled with the subsequent advocacy activities on the part of the women, has generated a greater level of mutual confidence on the part of both the official institutions and the less formal community groups. The women's new and growing ability to analyze problems emerging from their social situations has produced different perceptions of their daily reality, of their family and their social and political spaces. Thus the most important goal of the human rights education was to change the pre-existing attitudes and preconceptions of the women with respect to the concept of citizenship. To improve access to justice for female victims of violence, it was necessary to mobilize and to motivate the women to think of themselves differently, to make them more determined to take all the steps necessary to seek redress through community or state justice authorities. Once acquired, these changes in attitude carried over into the women's participation in other, larger social and political power structures.

While work remains to be done, there are a number of indicators of positive social change in the communities. At the top of the list is the consolidation of the administrative and organizational structure to assure the continued provision of services by the Defenders. They are now able to assure in a stable way the care and monitoring of cases, and the dissemination and promotion of rights through human rights education. They are also able to reach out to new communities where the human rights abuses caused by the indicators mentioned above, namely poverty, discrimination, illiteracy and limited knowledge of rights, are most prevalent. This outreach has meant that the percentage of reported cases of violence has increased. In other words, more victims are aware that the violence they are facing is remediable and thus have decided to begin to address it. This is very significant progress. It means that domestic violence is no longer as accepted as inevitable as it was in the past. This changed attitude has reduced the reason for the victims to feel guilty.

On the achievements of the Community Defenders, two defenders report:

> [...] At first we thought it was only about dealing with the formal case and then we could leave the victim to deal with it on her own. We soon saw that this was not all the case; the victim of violence needed us to support her much more, that we must stay with her. It was not enough to listen; rather, we should also enforce these women's rights before the authorities as ordinary people are very much afraid to speak. Then I realized that this approach opened many doors for us to promote a society which respected their rights, rights which previously were underestimated.
> (Toribio)

> I never imagined that the Office would work on cases; I thought that we would simply forward them.. But once we were working we saw that when the victims were sent to a government institution and were shuffled from one place to the next. They were not properly helped. So we realized we had to accompany them and monitor each case.
> (Constantine)

At a more personal level, these changes illustrate a better self-perception by victims, who now see themselves as citizens who enjoy rights (through the increase in their knowledge), possess an increased level of self-esteem (they feel they are heard), and have greater confidence in changing their lives for the better (they now want to participate in public affairs and institutions).

> We receive the victim who has come to request our services first by welcoming her. Then we provide the space for her to be calm, to relax and to explain the reason for her visit. We listen quietly, to establish a trusting relationship. After listening, we ask if the person is of age, what she wants to do, and how she wants to proceed. We listen again so that she can tell us everything that has happened and how long she has suffered abuse. Then we ask if her decision to file a complaint is firm, because many of the people who come to the Defenders just want to have their cases listened to or to ask us to visit their homes and speak with their partners.
> (Constantine)

The same goes for the Defenders who have gained greater confidence in their leadership skills and abilities. Their work has increased their social activism, and they have become more critical of what happens in their own political and social environments. Both the victims and the defenders are now heard in the public debates surrounding civil society and advocacy institutions. The following testimonies of some defenders are illustrative:

> [...] Then she says, "Do not be sad with your luck, you have to be strong." And she adds, "You know there will be workshops at the Defenders?" "What are the Defenders?" I asked. And she invited me to a workshop meeting in Urubamba. So I was interested, because I had studied the problem of human behavior (Anthropology), and said: "I must go there." So that is how I began to feel important; I felt good in the workshop. While we discussed certain topics, there appeared some terms and concepts that I had previously studied, so I said, "Why am I not practicing this?" There were ladies who participated, who raised their hands. I said, "What? I know these issues." But I did not participate; at that moment I felt a little inferior. Then I met with many of the ladies who were our fellow advocates and others who were lawyers, professionals.
>
> (Libertad)

> I learned a lot about the rights we have as human beings. But we also wanted something else: to be heard, to make the (men) see us as people, to prevent them from treating us as they sometimes do, like small things. In the training I realized that we were very valuable people, that we were really were worth much as women, children...
>
> (Manuela)

Changes of attitude within communities have mobilized more male supporters (originally the Defenders were almost all women), thus including men in the community who were willing to discuss problems rooted in the prejudices of male superiority. Human rights education has expanded the level of gender sensitivity, and there is also evidence of improved social peace and family harmony. One such case is that of Moses:

> [...] I was invited to participate in the First Regional Community Defense in Cusco. I did not know what to do; there were plenty of fellow participants, men and women who were all defenders. So immediately I took on that identity. Some do not understand what the Community Defenders are all about. There, they were speaking about how to protect children and the rights of women. Previously, that topic didn't occur; we only argued about community development, although there were many problems of family violence and child abuse. We can change our attitudes, but there are other people who do not care; it is not in their best interest because they only look after themselves and they don't share [...]. I am very excited to take this responsibility as an advocate, to meet and promote the rights. My fellow farmers have the same rights as any other citizen.
>
> (Moses)

There is plenty of evidence to show that Community Defenders have generated empowerment and leadership, especially on the part of women, by the confidence generated through their greater understanding and awareness of their own rights, and by their ability to identify problems and to effect change.

> The Defenders jolted me out of the passivity that had engulfed me and helped me get ahead by putting into practice what I've learned in the workshops. In conversations with organizations and contacts with the authorities, I no longer see them as people who are above me, but as people to whom I must report cases or situations that occur in our area.
> (Lucia)

This new consciousness has created a kind of movement, with structural changes resulting from new perceptions of gender roles within communities and within families. This has generated greater respect for the rights of women and increased attention to their demands by state judicial officers and other officials. Often, this change in attitude is directly related to the performance of the Defenders.

> The medical certificate is free, but often neither the nurses nor the issuers know it. Then we show our credentials and say, "Madam, good morning. I'm an advocate, and this is my credential. The certificate of family violence is free and you must issue it to this lady."
> "Ah, yes, yes," they say. "Have you brought the papers? What do you want?" So they treat us badly. The defenders do not react; they say, "One moment, miss. Good morning. We are community advocates who work to promote the rights and proper treatment of these women. We serve their cases and we forward them to the proper authority and you must politely and properly serve us." Then they finally say, "Oh, yes, yes," they calm down a bit and they serve us well—sometimes even kindly.
> (Constantine)

Greater coordination between community and state institutions has resulted in a willingness on the part of the state agencies to recognize the institutions of local communities as legitimate actors with whom it is beneficial to establish and maintain working relationships. By working with other advocates to create a greater consciousness of citizenship, the Defenders have acquired increased trust and effectiveness as social actors who are now heard and consulted by both private and public institutions. Human rights education has increased awareness and the internalization of rights. It has also led to an increase in confidence enabling women and others to identify and articulate their rights in their own words in public. They are, for example, now able to see that justice is on their side and that they can demand enforcement. Most importantly these advances are developing a societal momentum of their own which extends beyond the principal actors and activities.

The experience in Cusco illustrates how the intervention of an external educational agent like IDL can both bring about change and create a wider momentum within the target populations. The project won the ECLAC (Economic Commission for Latin America and the Caribbean) award in 2006, and IDL was invited to join the International Seminar on social innovation in Latin America and the Caribbean in November of 2010 on account of the success of the project. The achievements of the project have been enhanced by IDL's continuous monitoring of the process, notably progress and social changes as they appear, evaluating them and adjusting accordingly. This close attention has assured that the educational design and advocacy work are not based on an abstract idea of human rights, but on the specific needs and potential of each situation. In each community, IDL identified the specific situations in which these rights were being violated, and then the institutions where intervention could best influence the larger social fabric. Additionally, IDL paid close attention to introducing a gender perspective and discourse that would fit with the complex and challenging context of rural communities. The content of the human rights education had to take into account the differential social situations of families and individuals, rather than relying on a generic vision of a given population. The monitoring and adjustments, coupled with the education of state officials, has enabled the population to slowly acquire an understanding of the exercise of citizenship and of their rights. Little by little, the education has generated a more general change in attitudes and values in the direction of a more inclusive democratic culture and respect for human rights. For their part, officials have begun to recognize that they need to address the vulnerability and limitations of local populations and to prioritize the problems faced by women and children, the most vulnerable groups. Coordinating networks have been established, and the authorities now perform their functions better. In the process the rise in the political and social status of the Community Defenders and CODECC has obliged the state institutions to recognize them as legitimate actors and to see the necessity and benefits of establishing a more harmonious relationship between the demands of the population and the responses from the state and its agencies.

Conclusion

Among the obstacles to human rights education in Peru were, and continue to be, traditional cultural views of the place of women in society, illiteracy, difficult economic conditions, and weak if not corrupt government institutions. This study emphasizes the importance of designing a human rights education that (a) responds to real problems, not merely the communication of abstract ideas about human rights; (b) educates significant other actors simultaneously, in this case the local public officials; (c) builds partnerships with other institutions; and (d) ensures that the human rights learning is sustainable after the external inputs are withdrawn by working with established local groups, in this case the CDs. This study also shows how such education can have trickle-down benefits with respect to other social problems.

While progress has been made and the prospects are encouraging, the underlying historical discrimination facing rural populations, the deep cultural biases associated with machismo and high levels of corruption, among other problems, have not gone away and thus will require constant attention for the foreseeable future. However, the experience and results of the intervention are proof that social change is achievable through effective human rights education, and that sustainability through the institutionalization of this change is a viable goal.

Notes

1 A detailed report on the work of IDL in 2005 can be found at www.cepal.org/dds/innovacionSocial/e/proyectos/doc/DefensoriasComunitarias.Peru.esp.pdf.
2 They resulted in the following guiding principles:
> To assure access to justice for women and girls who are victims of violence and discrimination through an understanding of their rights and knowledge of which tools to demand. To encourage a more comprehensive judicial process that addresses the subjective and emotional dimensions involved in each case. To promote and exercise self-criticism with respect to the value systems, interests and goals of both external agents and the members of the local communities they sought to serve, and to empower rural women, enabling them to assume an active citizenship role and individual and collective participation in political and social affairs that affect their lives.

3 Law No. 26260 was adopted in December 1993. It was amended by Law No. 26763, adopted in March 1997.
4 World Health Organization, WHO Multi-country Study on Women's Health and Domestic Violence Against Women, www.who.int/gender/violence/who_multicountry_study/en/.
5 IDL no longer claims to be supporting these activities on its website (www.idl.org.pe/).

4 Human rights education in a secondary school in a conflict-torn region of Senegal

> Governments can play a key role in making the arguments for children's participation, highlighting the benefits this can bring at all levels of society. They should raise the matter in all public forums and with different audiences in order to convey a strong message that not only do children have a right to participate in all matters that affect them but that their active engagement brings clear and sustainable benefits.[1]

The conflict in Casamance

This study examines the use of HRE within a public school system even as a low-intensity conflict continues in the area. For over twenty years Casamance, a region of Senegal to the south of the Gambia and thus largely separate from the more developed northern region that includes Dakar, has been rocked by a persistent conflict between the Senegalese army and the Movement of Democratic Forces of Casamance (MDFC). The MDFC was formed in 1947 to seek independence for Casamance, or at least to obtain some degree of regional autonomy from the rest of the nation. In the 1980s the MFDC renounced the latter goal and advocated complete independence. On December 26, 1982, a group of MFDC militants raided the provincial capital of Ziguinchor and burned the national flag. A violent government crackdown followed, with the police arresting more than a dozen people including Father Diamacoune Senghor, the iconic leader of the MFDC.

In 1991, a peace agreement was signed to end the violence. Later that year, as part of the settlement, the Government of Senegal passed an amnesty law that granted all the MFDC fighters pardons for war crimes. However, peace has not come easily to the region. Over the ensuing two decades there have been frequent outbreaks of violence involving attacks and further crackdowns, followed by temporary ceasefires. In the early 1990s, human rights organizations not only denounced the acts of violence committed by members of the Senegalese military, but reported them to the African Human Rights Commission in the Gambia and the Human Rights Council in Geneva. Indeed, 2,000 such violations were reported just between 1996 and 1997.

The continuing bloody confrontations have caused massive displacements of native Senegalese to Guinea Bissau (around 6,000) and Gambia (approximately

7,000). National and international human rights organizations have denounced the arbitrary arrests, torture, and forced disappearances of Casamance residents that have resulted from the clashes between the MFDC militants and government soldiers, as well as the abuses committed against local civilians by members of the MFDC. The insecurity in southern Senegal was, and continues today, to be compounded by the use of landmines by the MFDC. This has led to a widespread abandonment of rice fields and orchards, the essential sources of livelihood for the people. Thus this low-intensity conflict has further intensified that poverty which has for so long brought so much suffering to the people of Casamance.[2]

In 2001 the newly elected national government in Dakar installed a new administration in Casamance. Another peace agreement was signed on December 30, 2004, and this led to the Foundiougne Negotiations of February 22, 2005. Nevertheless the low-intensity conflict persists in Casamance, with an increased level of violence in 2012.[3] Three factors have fueled the ongoing violence: a split within the MFDC between the northern-front fighters who favor disarmament and those on the southern front who do not; the emergence of a new armed movement called ATTIKA (the word for "warrior" in the Diola language) that is opposed to ending the conflict; and other fratricidal struggles in the southern region. While the country's many ethnic groups have coexisted relatively peacefully, inter-ethnic tensions between the Wolof people in the north and southern ethnic groups have played a significant role in the long-running Casamance rebellion, and at the center of the conflagration have been many grievous human rights abuses.

A host of local organizations have been established over the last two decades, all of them seeking to strengthen the capacity of Casamance's residents to respect and defend their rights. These include: the African Assembly for the Defense of Human Rights (RADDHO); the National Organization of Human Rights (ONDH); and Amnesty International-Senegal among others. These groups have been active organizing conferences, training workshops, and seminars on national human rights instruments; mobilizing; monitoring and documenting human rights abuses. Many locals have complained, however, that the educational activities sponsored by the NGOs are held too sporadically and rarely include provisions for follow up. The most obvious factor accounting for these deficiencies is the limited availability of international partners willing to provide the needed financial resources (Dieye 2010).

The role of human rights education in building peace

Instability is an ongoing feature of life in Casamance today, and most observers doubt that peace will come through the present path of low intensity conflict. The causes of this protracted conflict run deep in the region's political, social, economic, and cultural history, and thus the only possible long-lasting solution is one based on values rather than armaments. The aforementioned NGOs and in general other segments of civil society and of the international community, call for raising human rights consciousness among Senegalese and especially young people as they prepare to take on the responsibility of adult citizenship. More specifically, such actors see the region's surviving schools as the critical social institutions. By providing the Senegalese with a social space in which they can jointly apprehend the new political structures based on justice and human equality, the schools can slowly change the people's existing mentality of insecurity and fear into one of trust and mutual respect.

Senegal's educational leaders have indeed decided to make human rights education central to the new curricula now being introduced into all schools, not just in Casamance, but throughout Senegal. They have become part of the general international HRE movement, not least by participating in the activities associated with the UN Decade for Education in Human Rights (1995–2004). Senegal also has signed on to the Global Program for Education on Human Rights heeding its guidelines for countries wishing to adopt national HRE programs. Moreover, Article 1, Paragraph 2, of Senegal's Law of Orientation of Education legislates the nation's new commitment to provide its citizens with an education that is based upon human rights. The national education envisioned in this law seeks to promote the values upon which the nation is founded. It calls for an education that builds freedom, pluralist democracy, and respect for human rights. Beyond its calls for continual improvements in the areas of justice, fairness, and mutual respect, it provides, in effect, a moral and a civic mandate directing men and women to dedicate themselves to the common good by respecting the laws and rules of social life. Senegal also has ratified the UN Convention on the Rights of the Child (CRC), thereby obligating the Senegalese government to provide education in human rights widely, and to children. Still lacking, however, are the necessary programs for professionals working with and for children, raising their awareness about human rights, and training them to teach all aspects of the Convention.

It is widely recognized by ordinary citizens in Casamance that education must be directly targeted at bringing peace to the region. This chapter focuses on the Malick Fall Middle School in Ziguinchor, a town in the Casamance region, where the armed separatist movement is active. In and around Ziguinchor there have been numerous outbreaks of combat between MDFC and army soldiers as well as between MDFC factions, and several sweeps have been conducted by the army. MDFC rebels often commit highway robberies that make travel risky. Life is difficult for everyone in Casamance, and this means that the teachers experience on a daily basis, along with their students and the students' parents, physical insecurity caused by armed violence, food scarcity, and the continuing, substantial displacements of people moving from rural areas to urban centers like Ziguinchor, and to neighboring countries. The teachers interviewed for this study of the program at Malick Fall[4] continually underscored their belief in human rights education, for it allows them to base their teaching upon the actual problems that surround them, as they seek to change old, deeply engrained patterns of thinking and thereby slowly bring peace to the region.

The Human Rights Education Program at Malick Fall

Human rights NGOs have been recruited to assist Senegal's high school and college teachers in bringing HRE into their curricula. One such initiative has been implemented by CIVITAS, an international NGO that works in the field of citizenship and human rights education. In cooperation with the National Institute of Study and Action for Development Education (INEADE), CIVITAS-Senegal has carried out this project in collaboration with the Center for Civic Education (USA) and Senegal's Ministry of Education. The US Embassy in Senegal also has provided funding. The curriculum, *We the People: Project Citizen*, is modeled on CIVITAS-Senegal's Citizens Action Program (CAP) and has also borrowed elements of the curriculum used by Project Citizen, of the Center for Civic Education, in primary and secondary schools in the United States. Over the past ten years, CIVITAS-Senegal has introduced into more than a dozen Senegalese schools a democratic model of teaching and learning methods that emphasizes interactive, participatory, and inclusive practices and has incorporated into the curriculum the UDHR and other international human rights instruments. Like other organizations operating in Senegal and working for human rights, CIVITAS-Senegal partners with various local organizations and institutions as a way of grounding their efforts within the community, and thereby reaching a large percentage of its members.

In this case, the project has been operating in the middle school known as Malick Fall for six years. Students enter the CAP program as fourth graders and continue the work when they move on to the fifth grade. In the academic year 2009–2010, the program attracted 630 students. The teachers trained for this program chiefly teach social science subjects such as history and geography, but they are also responsible for teaching the classes that are at the program's core—civic education classes that explore issues of tolerance, conflict, solidarity, and social and economic development. In such classes a common HRE learning activity is to have the students work in groups to identify a public policy problem in their community. After the students have identified what they deem to be the most important problems in their communities, their teachers help them acquire the techniques they need to conduct accurate surveys and otherwise assemble data about their chosen topics. Each problem is deconstructed in the sense that the students, with the teacher's help brainstorm possible solutions, pick the best one and shape it as a public policy. They then create an action plan designed to convince local or state authorities to adopt their proposed policy.

At the end of each academic year the participants in CAP present their portfolio of work, which is a group articulation of their views on the topic, at a public hearing before a panel of civic-minded community members. The typical portfolio, a poster comprised of four panels, highlights the work done by the students over the course of the program. It directly reflects the classroom activities: brainstorming and identifying problems, learning about existing policy and legal frameworks, proposing solutions and arriving at viable action plans. In other words it is a summation of the students' acquired knowledge, conveyed by their own voices and with only minimal input from adults and thus teaching its own vital lesson about participation rights. The portfolio's four panels, into which the students typically incorporate topic-related newspaper clippings, statistics, interview transcripts, and articles, tend to take the following format:

- The first panel introduces a problem that affects the community and that can be addressed by enacting a public policy.
- The second panel is devoted to describing the various policies and laws that the state (Casamance, in this case) already has enacted to address the problem.
- The third panel presents the students' vision of new public policies that would better address they have identified.
- The fourth panel presents the student-generated action plan.

This method contrasts with the traditional curriculum. The CAP model requires students to learn about domestic public policy, relating local social and economic problems to international human rights standards. Providing ongoing support and training for the teachers involved in this new interactive pedagogy has been vital for its successful implementation. Throughout Senegal's history education has been conceived in strictly hierarchical terms, with the teacher being deemed the knowledge-keeper and the student the one who must tap into the teacher's knowledge, largely via rote-based memorization. Little wonder, given that they were expected simply to absorb the information provided to them by their teachers, that the children were not heard. Over the last decade, however, that outdated pedagogical approach has begun to be replaced by the new, more participatory and hence egalitarian one. The following extract is drawn from an interview with Ms. Cisse, a fourth-grade teacher at Malick Fall:

> There is a big change from the perspective of the first method. As we said, the traditional method is no longer valid, for it is interactivity that I have taken away from my experience in the CAP program but also from my own learning and from other seminars and workshops I have participated in. All of that has helped me to improve my class, mainly through activities: using icebreakers, role-playing, and so on.

The teachers' support for, and commitment to, the program have been a major reason for its success. As mentioned previously, the teachers interviewed by the researchers noted that interest in the program sprang directly from their often stressful daily experiences, which had led them to appreciate the need to take a human rights approach to education. Taken as whole, the school's teachers have come to see HRE as a powerful weapon in their ongoing battle against all forms of injustice. What they prize above all is the potential for HRE to instill good citizenship skills, based upon respect for rights and recognition of duties. At present the CAP program involves only a certain number of classes and teachers, but virtually every teacher we spoke with wants to see it extended to all of Malick Fall's classrooms.

The program's significance as a means of promoting children's educational and civic participation

> In education, schoolchildren are not systematically consulted in matters that affect them, and thus we recommend that governments should take further steps to promote, facilitate, and monitor systematic, meaningful, and effective participation of all groups of children in society, including in school.[5]

As we examined the CAP model we asked ourselves two questions: First, "in what ways is this program helping to advance the cause of children's participation?" And second, "how has the program helped children to think critically about the problems that affect their community?" In this section we study the CAP program in relation to its commitment to young people's participation rights and its recognition of children as a source of strength and opportunity for local communities, as opposed to merely a problem to be resolved. The participatory approach focuses on working with young people to identify the challenges they face within their communities, such as lack of opportunities for employment and recreation, lack of safe places to meet, and the negative attitudes of older people toward younger ones, or at least the former's inability, or unwillingness, to acknowledge the contribution the latter can make to their community. Respecting children's right to participate fully in their educational and civic lives not only empowers the children themselves, but thereby benefits their communities.

What also makes the CAP program supportive of children's rights is that it seeks not just to provide students with a theoretical course on human rights, but also to put them right at the center of the action. As the school's principal has put it: "The child is placed in the center of learning. Eventually the child participates in the construction of his own knowledge and skills" (Principal, interview with Ndour, 2010). The CAP-centric curriculum is relevant to students' daily lives. Human rights, standards, and skills are taught in ways that encourage students to apply them directly in the classroom by identifying and analyzing human rights violations in the surrounding society. Informational needs also are met, however, for students acquire information about those issues that affect them most closely and that they want to have their say about: freedom of expression and worship, the right to have a family, the right to obtain an education, the right to gender equality, the right to experience social solidarity within one's community, and the right to live in a healthy environment. Their new consciousness has resulted in the students wanting to remedy the violations they have identified in their school and their community, a point we will return to later.

The school has been transformed in nature, from one closed off to students, to one that takes their views into consideration. Everyone interviewed at Malick Fall said that the school is now far more conducive to open interactions between students and school officials. Children are acknowledged in the school as active participants, as evidenced by their increased ability to have their views heard by others. Teachers not only give much more weight to the students' views but they also have developed new types of questioning and are always seeking to give students opportunities to express their views. Teachers work to ensure that the views of a diverse range of children are sought, and that participation is not just afforded to the most outspoken children.

Below, one of the teachers, Ms. Badji describes how teachers, even those outside of the program, have become more patient, encouraging the children to voice their opinions, especially when they are working with students who, for whatever reason, do not easily express themselves.

> Before, I was a little too hard with the kids. For example, when a child was crying in class I did not even try to understand why, just putting him by the door for the rest of the class. But after this program I have started to manage the children's reactions, talking with them and understanding their problems. I now understand that a child may behave in a way that is not of his or her own volition. Overall this program has brought me closer to the children, and now we have good relations. Indeed, if someone among them has a problem, he or she comes to me and explains the problem, and I help him or her to solve it.

The new stance that the teachers have adopted toward their students has helped to create a climate of greater trust in the classroom, and schools that build trust and mutual respect among students and staff are implicitly rights-respecting. Such enhanced feelings of trust also bring better order and discipline for students. They began to voluntarily live the rules, as opposed to conceiving of them as merely externally imposed punishments for bad behavior. Classroom disruptions of course still occur, but if, for example, a fight breaks out between two students, it is predominantly their peers who intervene to restore order (Cisse, teacher, interview with Dieye, 2010). Given such examples of students becoming more responsible and motivated when they are treated as equals by adults, it comes as no surprise that so many of Malick Fall's teachers have not hesitated to adopt the new interactive and egalitarian approach.

At Malick Fall the appreciation of the new values grew within the student body as a result of the program. Everyone from the principal to the teachers pointed to changes in the students' behavior and attitudes and in the school's organizational activities.[6] Interviewees attributed these transformations to the pervasive new sense of respect for human rights and the fundamental principles of democracy. As the following interview extract shows, the principal is highly enthusiastic about the new pedagogical approach:

> It has enabled us to revise our rules regarding the operation of the school, and has brought to the forefront many aspects of education that formerly were ignored or at least not granted great importance. The keystone of the program is student participation in school life—that's what's important! Our

old daily habits revolved around the notion that the teacher was there to give knowledge—the student merely to take it. The CAP [program], with its central premise that the student has something to offer, has brought all of that old thinking into question. Now we think, "Just give students some responsibility, and you'll be amazed at the results!"

The HRE program has thus turned the school into a safe space where students' emotional needs are prioritized, where they are encouraged to engage in dialogue on subjects that matter a great deal to them, while developing a knowledge of human rights and an empathy for the victims of the human rights abuses committed in their communities. The success of the program can be measured in terms of the students' insights, their willingness to discuss sensitive topics openly, and their increased participation in the learning process. The impact of the program becomes apparent in both the students' artwork and in the enthusiastic remarks about the program which permeated the interviews with students, teachers, and the alumni.

Impact assessment: critical thinking, empathy, and civic responsibility

One clear theme that emerges through the students' artwork is their feeling of compassion and civic responsibility. Through their participation in the program these young people have clearly forged a firm grasp on human rights problems. They are especially aware of the issues affecting other children in their communities, most notably those children who do not attend school and who live in the streets of their town. Their drawings depicting street children, child soldiers, and child laborers implicitly attest to their new found ability to identify cases in which children's rights have been violated and their shared comments make it explicit. For instance, a child in the fourth-grade class who had drawn a picture of a child working told the researcher: "We must say no to child labor." Another student expressed her concern that most people turn a blind eye to street children, adding that such children deserve to be cared for by the government. She summed up her thoughts in a poem she wrote:

> Do you see this wretched being working on the streets?
> This being is a child
> A child is a treasure! And
> Treasures we must care for
> Work? Yes! But it is not for everyone
> Would it be out of spite? No!
> A child has done nothing wrong
> Out of ignorance? No
> The man has done nothing out of ignorance
> This creature has done nothing to deserve such treatment
> Help him to live happily.

The students' visual and written materials such as drawings, photographs, and poems were created as a means to both express their ideas and insights and make conscious connections with basic human rights concepts. The cited poem not only tells us how sensitive the students in the program have become to their surroundings, in this case to their obligation to other children, but also reminds us of their ability to use words and images to concretize and internalize their new-found understanding of rights and rights violations.

A good number of the drawings depict street children begging all day long through the streets of the city, barefoot and poorly dressed—conditions which the students clearly believe constitute an affront to human dignity, for they often told their teachers that such children should be in school, not out on the streets. To underscore their conviction that the government must implement measures to protect street children by providing them with alternatives to begging, they have drawn public buildings such as courthouses and police stations, noting in their comments that these institutions exist precisely in order to fight back against rights violations (Dieye 2010).

One student's drawing depicts one of the all-too-numerous street children known as "talibes." Talibes are children who have been committed to the care of religious institutions or Koranic Schools, often by their parents because of their own poverty, but who nonetheless spend many hours every day on the streets, begging for funds to support the institution. Such children are especially at risk because they are easy prey for recruiters of armed groups. In the following caption, a child describes her drawing:

> Woman! Don't you see this sadness on the street? This child who starves, who dies of thirst
>
> Who walks barefoot, who has no place to sleep, who has no one to console him
>
> What do you do for him, who never for a day feels happy, who is always miserable, beaten, ignored?
>
> Take pity. Help him survive.

The profound impact that the conflict in Casamance has had upon its children's imaginations is also well illustrated by a drawing that shows an adult handing a weapon to a child while promising lots of gifts so as to convince him that he is wasting his time by going to school. The drawing is accompanied by this poem that reflects the despair felt by so many of Casamance's children who have seen their youth ebbing away, ever since the outbreak of the conflict:

> We, the young, we live in a world of turmoil, hatred, undermined by all these wars. We have tried it all, we pray, we cry.
>
> The beauty of youth is no longer visible, this voice is not heard anymore
>
> We pray that peace returns to this country, to our Senegal
>
> That young people can be free, that youth can smile again, that the sounds of youth are heard once more.

In addition to poetry and drawings the students' portfolios also contain photographs that are vivid depictions of the human rights violations going on outside their school. The results constitute an impressive articulation of their understanding of the rights to live and to study in a healthy, safe place. Some of those photos reveal the dilapidated state of the Malick Fall school, its walls stripped bare and half collapsed, which for the students symbolizes a deficiency in physical safety and thereby in academic promise. Moreover, in the pictures they have taken of the dirty public places of their city, such as the marketplace in Ziguinchor, the students convey the message that garbage coexisting so closely with the selling of food attests to the failure of the local authorities to ensure the well-being of the people. Our own sense in this regard has been confirmed by Covell and Howe in their research on children's rights education in Canadian schools.[7] Such images are not only acting as a stimulus to the development of rights respecting attitudes, but are evoking a strong empathy from the students that they then channel into their analyses of social justice problems such as poverty, discrimination, and lack of government accountability.

One of the children's photographs shows a memorial site that was erected by the state of Senegal in commemoration of the Joola shipwreck that occurred in September 2002. The tragedy killed over 1,500 people, most of them residents of Casamance. The student photographers said that it is important for the community to have as many reminders of this tragedy as possible, not only because they believe it was brought on by the government's lack of commitment to transport people safely, but also because so many of them lost a parent, a friend, or a neighbor in the shipwreck.

In summary, these representations which have resulted from the children's learning about their community in its relation to human rights, demonstrate the CAP program's highly positive impact upon them. Such learning has been constructed out of both their own lived experiences and their empathetic, art-enabled glimpses into the lives of others, especially of children whose lives have been equally, or even more deeply ravaged, by the conflict that has engulfed Casamance throughout their lives. Their schooling has invited them to think of themselves as active citizens, and of human rights as tools at their disposal as they seek to effect social change. Each poem, drawing, and photograph demonstrates how the student can share with the viewer the human rights-related insights that he or she possesses. More broadly, these artistic opportunities have also given them a sense of what it means to possess their own personalized knowledge. It is also worth noting that the artistic method which is used to evaluate the understanding of children about their rights and the rights of others shows that learning can never adequately be gleaned through just questions and answers. The artwork and the portfolios can and should be seen as expressions of the children's urge to become full citizens. They also remind us, however, that the classroom has become a safe, nurturing space within which the young people of Casamance, who daily endure the poverty and instability that continues to characterize their region can address their real-life concerns, even as they imagine a better life for themselves and for those other children who are struggling to cope with life as it rages on, outside the walls of the Malick Fall school.

Sustainability

In keeping with other studies of the impact of children's rights education, we found evidence in the Malick Fall fourth- and fifth-graders of child-initiated attempts to actively redress the rights violations of other children. However, we wanted to obtain a longer-term view of what becomes of the knowledge and skills acquired by those students who have participated in the CAP program, and we were able to do so by eliciting feedback from five former students who had participated in 2003 and 2004. In their responses to a questionnaire, these CAP alumni told us how the program had altered their thinking and how their new rights-awareness is shaping their current lives. These five students were among the first to participate in the program at Malick Fall in 2003, a time marked by an upsurge in violence when the conflict was still far from being reduced through negotiation and consultation. Thus the conflict itself served as the educational focus of their studies. The students told us that in addition to gaining a better understanding of the conflict—both its origins and its disastrous impact on people through population displacement, loss of life, destruction of property, and abandoned schools—they also learned about human rights, its history and its inverse relation to these tragedies.

The responses to the questionnaire showed that these former students had retained their skills with respect to both presentation of self and participant-observer research, notably through their interviewing strategies and their appreciation of the need for both creativity and collaboration. Unfortunately, however, all of them were unable to integrate their findings and proposals into public affairs. At the time Casamance was still facing significant difficulties following one of the most virulent periods of the conflict. Some seven years after their graduation, none of the alumni were involved in activities related to human rights and none had sought to develop strategies to implement and sustain peace-building actions.

All of the interviewed alumni expressed great regret that they were not using much of what they had learned at Malick Fall in their jobs or their lives (Dieye 2010). This cannot help but be a cause for concern, given the CAP program's implicit mandate to provide the next generation of Casamance citizens with the knowledge and skills they will need to bring lasting peace to the region. The fact is, the program has not set up a mechanism designed to extend its short-term educational gains over the long term. Hence the need for the program to create a pool of mentors or tutors with whom the program's alumni can work after they leave Malick Fall. Such a system would serve to keep alumni informed about human rights initiatives via their meetings with their mentors and their participation in advocacy groups in the community and beyond. The goal would stay precisely the same: to link classroom learning with the policy and social changes going on in the community outside. Ultimately, school officials working in collaboration with NGOs in the region will incorporate both students and alumni's suggestions into the strategies of the various organizations working in post-conflict reconstruction.

Conclusion

Today in Casamance the conflict remains unresolved. Inside one middle school in Malick Fall, however, students continue to learn about human rights. The sheer existence of this program shows that schools are capable of becoming places within which communities can build a base of support for a democratic way of life predicated on a sense of fairness and equality and a respect for human beings and human dignity. The critical factor is that those who run the school's CAP program have taken seriously the view that children are rights-holders and citizens. That schools are democratic communities where children learn the values and practices of citizenship, and that educating children about their basic human rights, including their right to participate in all matters affecting them, is a legal obligation.

Senegal's Minister of Education has reiterated the need to integrate courses in international human rights law into the curricula of all the nation's schools. The nation's overarching goal is to build on the reform plan for civic education, based upon human rights, that was adopted by the Ministry of Education in 2008. State-run schools are legally obligated to educate children about their basic human rights, including their right to participate in all matters affecting them. It is now up to school officials to implement HRE in other schools in the region, especially in ways that allow students' voices to be heard. The government also must understand that learning for, and about human rights, is truly effective only when the learners can channel what they have learned into their direct participation in public life.

Notes

1 Every child's right to be heard: a resource guide on the rights of the child general comment no 12. www.unicef.org/adolescence/files/Every_Childs_Right_to_be_Heard.pdf. Save the Children UK, 1 St John's Lane London EC1M 4AR UK.
2 For more information on the conflict in Casamance see http://pdf.usaid.gov/pdf_docs/PDACI085.pdf.
3 For more on this please see "New displacement and challenges to durable solutions in Casamance," www.internal-displacement.org/8025708F004CE90B/(httpCountries)/934E69452D825EE5802570A7004B70B1?OpenDocument.
4 In 2010, Aminata Dieye conducted semi-structured interviews with five teachers and the principal of the school, and engaged in group work with approximately 43 students, although around a hundred students had expressed eagerness to participate in the assessment activities. Working with the chosen 20 girls and 23 boys (insisting on parity), all of whom had participated in the CAP program for a minimum of six months, our researcher developed an assessment tool using visual representations of human rights as a way to test what the students had learned. This method was predicated on the notion that much can be learned by both teachers and students through the

careful analysis of the representations of human rights which the students provide in their drawings, photographs, and poems. Follow-up interviews with the participants were conducted in small groups by the researchers, followed by semi-structured interviews with alumni of the school in order to arrive at a deeper understanding of impact. The students who participated in the study were divided into two groups. Members of the larger group were broken up into five working subgroups of seven or eight students. Each student was asked by the researcher to draw pictures and then to write poems or captions that would symbolically capture some aspect of their environment which embodies human rights or a significant breach thereof. The smaller group of four students was sent to take photographs because they all had proficiency in that area. All of the students were between 15 and 17 years old and had attended at least one of the CAP courses. The two teachers (who were members of the three-person research team) involved in the program helped the lead researcher to organize the students and the latter to complete their assignments. Next all three researchers asked two former CAP participants, who are now in their freshman year at the local high school in Djignabo, to analyze these HR-related pictures that younger students at their former school had taken. Their evaluation of the younger children's drawings was designed to assess the level of understanding and awareness of students who have recently completed the program. To that same end the research team sent a questionnaire to five former students who had attended Malick Fall and participated in CAP during 2003 and 2004.
5 Every child's right to be heard: a resource guide on the rights of the child general comment no 12. www.unicef.org/adolescence/fifiles/Every_Childs_Right_to_be_Heard.pdf. Save the Children UK, 1 St John's Lane London EC1M 4AR UK.
6 Other authors who have written about the impacts of human rights education with public schools include the following: Monisha Bajaj has examined the impact of human rights education in school in the Dominican Republic. See Bajaj, "Human rights education and student self-conception in the Dominican Republic." *Journal of Peace Education*, *1*(1), March 2004. Rosa Mujica has studied the implementation of human rights education program in Cusco Peru. See Mujica's "Que nos enseñen bonito: El trabajo en derechos humanos y equidad de género en escuelas rurales de Quispicanchi, Cusco," Instituto Peruano de Educacion en Derechos Humanos y la Paz, Lima 2009. And finally, Katherine Covell, Brian Howe, and Justin McNeil's important work in Hampshire England. See "Implementing children's human rights education in schools" in *Improving Schools*, *13*(5), 117–132 July 2010.
7 Covell, Katherine and Brian Howe, 1999.

5 Never again
The Master's degree in human rights in Lima, Peru

The conflict and the Institute

> Peru's history contains more than one difficult, embarrassing, period of genuine national prostration. None of them, however, deserves to be marked so indelibly with the seal of the shame and dishonor as a fragment of history we are forced to replay in these pages. The two last decades of the twentieth century are—it must be put bluntly—a mark of horror and disgrace to the State and Peruvian society.

These are the words of Dr. Salomón Lerner Febres who presided over the Truth and Reconciliation Commission (TRC) of Peru between June 2001 and August 2003. In the preface to the first edition of the *Hatun Willakuy*, an abbreviated version of the Final Report of the Peruvian TRC, Dr. Lerner wrote that the decades of 1980 to 2000 witnessed a situation of unprecedented violence in Peru, which left "a painful account of killings, abductions, forced disappearances, torture, unjust imprisonment, and serious crimes and human rights violations."[1] The conflict was marked by numerous armed confrontations between the forces of the Peruvian Communist Party, the Shining Path and the Tupac Amaru Revolutionary Movement on the one hand, and the Peruvian state on the other.

Examining these terrible events, researchers found a lack of preparation and knowledge about human rights, both within the institutions of the state and among ordinary citizens. Some Peruvians protested and tried to use the existing legal and institutional mechanisms to complain about the human rights violations that occurred during the period of violence. Dr. Lerner identified the violence and violations as one of the reasons for the absence of professionals able to integrate the theory and practice of human rights into their work, let alone transmit their knowledge to others. Universities in Peru had not allocated any resources to human rights studies in either graduate or undergraduate education. In response the Institute for Democracy for Human Rights (IDEH) and the MA program in human rights at the Pontificia Universidad Cathólica del Perú (PUCP) emerged to address this need.

The Institute uses the following five cross-cutting and interrelated frames of reference as the basis for its analyses, needs assessments and planning for all its projects:

66 *The Master's degree in human rights in Peru*

1 Access to justice. To promote democratization it needs to develop more of a multicultural character. This calls for normative, legislative and institutional changes that incorporate international standards in human rights into domestic law as well as into legislative and judicial practice.
2 Political reform. This theme examines the party system, the structure of governance and citizenship in the current post-conflict situation. It focuses on the impact of such challenges and opportunities in the political system such as the obligations and limitations of citizenship, access to justice, the impact of culture and its institutional representation.
3 Exclusion and discrimination. As evidenced by the TRC Final Report, this frame of reference recognizes that in Peru it is impossible to promote democracy and the rule of law without recognizing the presence of ethnic discrimination. To fight ethnic and other forms of discrimination, it is necessary to identify and analyze the limits of public policies and to promote the implementation of institutional reforms designed to respond to the injustices that result from discrimination. This calls for studies of the old and new forms of violence that result from and cause social exclusion, especially where the institutional actions of the State are involved.
4 Collective memory. This frame of reference addresses the long-standing controversies in Peruvian society that transcends the effects of a 20-year armed conflict. IDEH is therefore studying the processes associated with collective memory within Peruvian society, in particular the creation and cultivation of public spaces for memory and their impact on reconciliation. To this end, the Institute also sponsors social, cultural and artistic events that relate to violence and post-conflict processes.
5 Educational reform. The fifth frame of reference is based on IDEH's belief that the study, understanding, and reform of the educational system are fundamental to the consolidation and dissemination of a democratic culture, as well as to the promotion of the values of peace and social justice. In this task, educators play an important role and it is imperative to strengthen their legitimacy in the development of national education. Implementing these goals, however, requires the formation of a quantum mass of professionals committed to defending and promoting democracy and human rights and their enforcement in the economic and political institutions of the nation. To strengthen theoretical and practical knowledge in these fields at all levels of society, IDEH has, for example, instituted a number of academic training programs for professors and students, as well as short training courses for professionals whose responsibilities involve human rights and human rights abuses.[2] Among the first of these programs was the Master's degree in Human Rights.

The design, implementation, and execution of the Master's degree in Human Rights at PUCP is based on the principle that academic spaces are necessary to identify and promote the conceptual knowledge, analytical, and critical skills as well as operational tools that Peru needs to prevent a return to the violence of the last two decades of the twentieth century. PUCP believes that superior scholarship on the part of its faculty members is an essential contribution to this task. Moreover, as noted above by Dr. Lerner, the scholarship must address the void in Peruvian universities in specialized and systematic training in the protection of democratic values and human rights. In his words,

> one of the topics not addressed in the [Final TRC] Report but which was understood to be a problem was the fact that although human rights are inherent in every human being, seeking to understand their full meaning, as opposed to its use in popular discourse and to token respect, does not galvanize a large following, at least in Peru. What I mean is as follows: we Peruvians talk about human rights and some even talk a lot about these rights, but we do not know what they are; we do not know how to defend them; and we do not know how to respond when those rights are threatened. Moreover, I realized that this is true in my own university, a place where rights could be studied more systematically, not just in a course in the Faculty of Law or through allusions in the odd course in philosophy.[3]

In Dr. Lerner's eyes, the fact that Peru lacked a center of higher learning in human rights demonstrated and reinforced the lack of both interest, and professional expertise on the part of Peruvian society. This perception is reinforced by a professor who teaches the course "Multiculturalism and Human Rights" in the program. He states:

> In our country, human rights have a serious problem of low social legitimacy. I have always wondered why, when the human rights groups in our country are active and actually do a great job, their size and influence are minimal relative to the population as a whole and to the seriousness of the human rights problems that exist and face Peru.[4]

The Master's degree in Human Rights at PUCP was inaugurated in March 2004. To respond to demand for human rights graduate programs elsewhere in the country in 2007, the Institute developed the Decentralized Diplomas in Human Rights in the departments of Ayacucho, Arequipa, Puno, Ancash, Cajamarca and Trujillo. In August 2009 it also adopted a virtual or distance-learning mode of the degree to promote the spread of the topics covered in the program by involving participants from different cities and different backgrounds who were unable to reside in or come to the city of Lima. The Master's degree also works directly with the Master's degree in Fundamental Rights program at Madrid's Universidad Carlos III enabling students to complete their MA in Spain.

The core components of the Master's degree in human rights

The curriculum of the Master's degree at PUCP is comparable to the offerings of inter-disciplinary MAs at other universities in the US and Europe. It offers a selection of courses that enable students to prepare themselves for the human rights challenges in different prospective careers in public policy, social services, education and public health, but also in corporate social responsibility, peacebuilding and environmental rights.

While there may be no single core curriculum for such a varied set of educational needs, the MA program identifies the following as important intellectual content: the international human rights framework, different forms of human rights advocacy, conflicts between international standards and local culture and practice, and problem-solving skills to address a variety of conflicts. A second range of skills are those required to transpose international and abstract standards into local language, law, institutions and culture, in ways that are sustained by the local population and local officials. A third range of skills common to all human rights work and needed by the different professions is the ability to analyze the economic and social forces and institutions at work, especially those thought to have brought about the civil conflict. Linked to this analysis are the insights, research, and methodologies needed to delineate the remedies needed to reduce past abuses and support a future peaceful and productive society.

The program has identified three key components or goals: (1) the enrollment of a diverse student body of professionals capable of having a multiplier effect; (2) an interdisciplinary curriculum; and (3) linking HR theory and practice. The first component for the MA program is to enroll a diverse student body with substantial multiplier potential, namely young professionals seeking careers where they would encounter human rights problems on a daily basis. These include members of the legal and law enforcement professions, teachers, members of the clergy, social workers, the providers of other social and humanitarian services, and especially the many government officials who administer public services. Moreover, given Peru's history, members of Peru's military were also seen as part of the target population. Those attending from these groups already have a university degree, and are thus prepared for an intensive advanced course in human rights studies. It was also expected that in both their professional and private lives, graduates of the program would integrate their new human rights consciousness into their daily lives as citizens.

The enrollment of women in the Master's program is twice as high as that of men. As more women obtain higher education, more will be able to occupy positions as specialists, executives, managers, and professors. This trend puts women in a better position to address patriarchy and the problems associated with the high levels of violence in Peru. Also, nearly half of the students are between the ages of 20 and 29. Their youth and expectations bring dynamism and stimulate interaction with those who do not belong to the same generation but share common interests.

The program owes much to the institutional support it receives from the University. PUCP, however, is a private university that charges fees to its students. Access to external financial support for fellowship has been difficult, meaning that poorer students are not able to attend, and some who begin to attend later drop out when they can no longer afford the fees or the lost income due to the demands of study. Thus although the MA program is relatively cost-effective in that it demands few additional resources, the fees can remain an obstacle to enrolling a diverse student body.

Recently the program has provided scholarships to nine students in the traditional and distance-learning tracks of the program. This funding comes from Misereor, a foundation affiliated with the German Catholic Church. The scholarships are distributed by a selection committee made up of professors on the basis of academic qualifications and economic need. These scholarships are a particularly important support for the virtual module of the program, as the majority of those students are from regions other than Lima, where average incomes are lower, but where the toll during the years of armed violence was the highest, and therefore where access to professionals specialized in human rights is most needed. Students who are unable to complete the two-year program due to financial or other reasons and pass the first two semesters receive a Graduate Diploma in Human Rights. Another certificate that shows that students have completed 50 percent of the program can be used to improve their employment opportunities. It also allows them to return and complete the program.

An important future objective of the MA program is outreach to professionals and ordinary citizens who do not work in the human rights field. The Institute follows closely the work of some of its graduates interested in reaching these different groups. It is also concerned with the limited enrolment of students in fields other than law. For example, a professor in the program points to the need to reach members of the armed forces. Given the training they receive in combat environments and the work they do in society, he argues:

> A latent but necessary task is to assess public awareness with respect to human rights. How many people, for example, consider it an important, vital, national, political concern? How many of the graduates from this program can make use of their training in other sectors. It would also be useful to follow up with the military personnel that have completed the Master's. How can media and communications be better used to reach the sectors without an appreciation of human rights?

IDEH believes that expanding the range of professions among its MA students is linked to the role of multidisciplinary studies as the only way to guarantee a better understanding of international human rights in theory and practice among the citizenry at large. Graduates of the program are encouraged to share their experience at IDEH to promote other interdisciplinary projects. Remaining in contact with and supporting alumni projects will permit IDEH to learn which elements of the program can be improved.

The second core component and goal is an interdisciplinary human rights curriculum. Unlike a law program, an interdisciplinary curriculum was chosen in order to respond to the width of perspective of the future political and economic political development of their country. Structured as a program of interdisciplinary education and training, the MA is designed to promote dialogue among the various disciplines that deal with democracy and human rights. This counteracts the notion that human rights are a matter that relates only to the law. A professor in the program expressed it as follows:

> I've always wondered why students who are not in law school are not interested in the issue of human rights and the truth is that I have yet to find the answer. Why is the issue of human rights a legal issue and isn't also seen as an educational issue, an anthropological theme, a historical subject, a philosophical issue?

The virtual modes of the Master's degree follow the same interdisciplinary curriculum. In Dr. Lerner's words:

> It is not merely a matter of law school or branch of law, but we, as is well known, have an interdisciplinary curriculum. First, we accept not only those who have completed law, but also those who studied sociology, anthropology, etc. and we have, therefore, an entire philosophical, psychological, gender, economic perspective, because human rights are rights, yes, but they are human, and human life in society implies, involves sexuality, involves the economy, implies education, it involves health. Then, of course is "all-embracing," to put it that way or the approach should be focused, in fact, on the studies that we conduct here as part of the Master's degree.

This interdisciplinary approach is reinforced by the diverse disciplines and backgrounds of the professors and students. In the classroom, interdisciplinary academic dialogue shows how different angles can and must identify and define remedies for human rights problems. The discussions and debates draw on legal, anthropological, economic and educational research to understand and manage different theories and interpretations of human rights in theory and in practice. Students also bring to bear their own real-life experiences. In addition to the exchange of ideas and experience and on a more practical note, classroom exchanges have also resulted in proposals for external funding and student group collaboration in community advocacy and mobilization.

A graduate of the Master's program in Human Rights, who is now a professor in the MA program, states:

> My expectations were largely met. First, the M.A. allowed me to address human rights from a perspective of philosophy, sociology, history, economics, and politics, among others, which has proved extremely useful for developing my work. This interdisciplinary dimension, moreover, is not only present in the professor-student relationship, but also among the students, who come from different disciplines, enrich the debate with questions, comments and arguments that often one does not bring up.

The interdisciplinary focus of the program has been appreciated by the participating professors. They valued the approach itself, learning from and about students outside their own field. In the words of one of the program's professors:

> Now, for me it has been a new experience because I never had experience teaching about human rights issues ... Instead, I had experience of working on human rights issues with peasant leaders, with the native population, but not at a graduate level. [In addition] (...) there is always the presence of foreign students who come here. So in that sense, I think so, (...) that the vision I had of human rights has been greatly enriched by the contributions the students themselves bring ... I would not know about all the famous resolutions that have emerged from the Inter-American Court on issues of indigenous peoples' rights. And of course, what is happening in Colombia and what not. And that is in part not just through contact with students, but also with some professors.

Interaction among faculty members from different disciplines has increased academic collaboration, interdisciplinary research and joint publications which in turn enrich both the MA in Human Rights and the culture of human rights in Peru.[5] Faculty from the MA program have collaborated with faculty from other universities inside and outside Peru to enrich scholarship on human rights.

On a practical level, finding remedies for social conflict and human rights abuses requires a more sophisticated analysis of the causes of social conflict than a MA program in human rights can offer on its own. Devising effective solutions for the complex social situations and human rights abuses in countries like Peru requires the resources of different academic disciplines, of different professions and of different international and national institutions. Thus one great value of interdisciplinary programs is the interaction they encourage among future professionals who will create the political and economic institutions necessary to solve inevitable social conflicts.

A third core component or goal of the MA program is to recognize the importance of linking human rights theory and practice. At the conclusion of the degree, the graduates will have acquired the ability to apply the theoretical and practical tools to human rights practice, enabling them to respond appropriately to situations that arise in their professional and private lives. One student, an educator and first-year graduate, expected "to receive a theoretical and methodological training on human rights," and was very satisfied with the program's achievement of this objective. Similarly, a student states that

> [my] first expectation of the program was that such training would extend my knowledge in the field of human rights and the management of international standards, and would also train me to advise the indigenous organizations in the proposed draft of indigenous laws and the design of public policies to be included within the policies of the State.

In question is how learning in a university brings about desired social change. Within the field of human rights education, educators typically subscribe to the line of thinking characterized by Paulo Freire as problem-solving and critical analysis rather than a model designed merely as the acquisition of new knowledge. At PUCP this model is implied in the various characteristics outlined above. For example by bringing disciplines together and seeking a diverse student body PUCP wants the students and their instructors to address the inevitable discrepancies among their various definitions and findings. By also emphasizing the link between theory and practice the program is seeking to overcome traditional, largely deductive and expert- or principle-based academic thinking. Rather the goal of the Master's program is to show the students how the resources of the various disciplines in conjunction with the human rights perspective can be used to address the challenges facing Peru today. Its educational strategy is to expose students to methods of applied research, to create spaces for dialogue, and to undertake a systematic analysis of public policies in the light of human rights and the obligations of the state.

Impact assessment

Conceived in the wake of Peru's TRC, led by Dr. Lerner, the MA program was designed to help prevent another period of major human rights abuses by strengthening democracy and the observance of human rights throughout Peru. In pursuit of the commitment to *nunca más*, "never again," the program now provides academic and professional training in human rights for the young Peruvians who were in, or would go on to private and government service, and who planned to use their professional responsibilities to strengthen democracy and the observance of human rights in Peru. The impact of the program should be measured in terms of its effectiveness in producing professionals who not only integrate human rights principles and practices into their professional work but also encourage and teach others to do so.

Of the ten students and former students interviewed for this study, seven were working in institutions that focus on human rights. Three others were self-employed but address human issues in their daily work. They now work in the following professional fields: electoral and democracy education, legal practice in human rights law, and poverty alleviation.

Several alumni report that they have managed to introduce the human rights approach into their professional work, thus spreading the principles that had studied. The police colonel, for example, describes some of his accomplishments in the police force as follows:

> The social structure in the police department is very vertical and hierarchical. Nevertheless, the discussion of human rights gave me the opportunity to promote an educational project without generating tensions within the department. These tensions could easily have occurred because educational projects often, shall we say, are manipulated by the authoritarian leaders for

their own ends. This did not happen in the case of the human rights training. The skills that I learned enabled me to organize capacity building courses within the department and to train additional instructors to promote human rights education throughout the police department. This was especially successful beginning in the year 2000, following an agreement of cooperation between the national police and the Red Cross.

The impact of the program on these professionals cannot be fully explored here, but their knowledge is altering the culture of the institutions in which they now work. This is only a very first step on the road, for example, towards Lerner's goal of a popular as well as a professional and governmental knowledge and commitment to human rights strong enough to prevent another national conflict. The level of achievement outlined here is modest given the size of the challenge, namely a country with an ethnically diverse population of about 30 million where the majority does not participate in the modern economy and polity. The program is only too aware of the size of the challenge it faces.

The challenges

A fundamental challenge for the MA program is to attract students from Peru's indigenous communities which have historically been excluded from the Peruvian mainstream. They remain in a vulnerable position vis-à-vis the country's ruling, commercial, and urban populations. Its members lack the theoretical and practical tools to claim and defend their rights within the political and social structure of modern Peru. The expertise in human rights that has been acquired by one of its members though the MA program will provide some tools to these communities. The urgent need is to expand the reach of human rights education programs to include more *awajún* community members and other native and indigenous communities.

The second challenge is the lack of attention to gender in the courses. The challenge is to expand teaching and research on the protection of women's human rights in Peru. Like the first challenge, this challenge is substantial because few professors and students are in a position to study in-depth problems as critical, diverse and complex as the direct and indirect discrimination that victimizes women in Latin America and undermines their ability to participate actively in the public sphere, and to protect and exercise their rights. In Peru, the gender gap within the indigenous communities poses a range of truly major challenges. The conflict and continuing post-conflict tensions have had an especially adverse impact on women. Indigenous women have been victims of human rights abuse in multiple ways by both state and non-state actors. They and their children also suffer from the structural violence caused by endemic poverty. Public policies in Peru have yet to recognize and respond to abuses consequent to gender. This challenge is also addressed in the study in this volume on women in Cusco, Peru.[6]

The third challenge is to attract students from more of the key sectors, notably from the domestic and international commercial and corporate world, the media, the military and police as well as the clergy, all of which are influential forces in the country as a whole. Also missing so far among the students are primary and secondary school teachers. They are especially important multipliers of human rights understanding. As one professor put it: "[O]ne question that lingers is, what capacity do we have to reach those people who aren't already the people who believe in these things?"

Future direction: distance learning

IDEH recognizes the need to reach larger sections of the population. Accordingly it is now expanding its training programs in human rights through the use of distance learning for the decentralized or off-campus diploma, and by creating a special unit on women's rights. The diploma is based on courses using distance-learning technologies and taught by PUCP professors as well as professors from other Andean and Spanish universities. This innovation permits Peruvian and other students to share a virtual classroom and to exchange academic and professional experiences. The Decentralized Diplomas in Human Rights are now available in the provinces of Ayacucho, Arequipa and Puno with the support of the World Bank. The government of the Netherlands is funding the program in the provinces of Ayacucho (hardest hit by the conflict), Trujillo, Cajamarca and Huaraz. This, IDEH's first experience in decentralized educational activity, has been free of charge to the participants. Like the Master's program, the design and implementation of these diplomas are interdisciplinary and organized to meet the empowerment needs of civil society. The goal of the diploma program is the development of academic knowledge and practical skills in human rights. The target group is professionals from a variety of different backgrounds. IDEH seeks to satisfy the immediate learning needs and demands of those professionals working in the economically marginalized areas of the country.

The decentralized diplomas in these seven locations have trained 280 professionals without their having to move from their place of residence, enabling them to apply the knowledge as they acquired it in their professional lives. Each lasting two months the diploma programs are a synthesis of the main theoretical and practical subject matters covered in the Master's in Human Rights at the PUCP. Thus, these programs are seen as another way to disseminate and multiply the benefits and impact of the Master's in Human Rights program itself.

The format and content of each diploma program are designed to meet the specific needs and demands of professionals from civil society in each region. This calls for adaptation to their learning abilities conditioned as they are by the overall social marginalization and limited economic and educational opportunities characteristic of the regions in question. Evaluation research by IDEH found that the diploma program met a real need on the part of the target population, reflecting the major gap in knowledge of human rights in rural areas compared with the capital Lima.

Finally one major challenge that has to be addressed is the validity of the assumption that human rights education and a more general culture of human rights within a society can prevent future violence. The evidence to support this assumption in the Peru program is still being accumulated. Certainly it helps if people believe that a human rights culture can prevent violence. Second there is increasing evidence elsewhere in Peru that past training programs in human rights have reduced, inter alia, domestic violence. Some of the graduates of the IDEH Master's also testify to the positive social impact of their learning and skills. Nevertheless implicit in much of the evidence in this and the other studies in this book is the fact that human rights education is not a stand-alone activity. It has to be buttressed by other social forces. At the top of that list is remunerative employment. This is an important challenge and is part of the IDEH ongoing reflection and planning.

Conclusion

This study shows how a university-based program can respond to the need for social change through the creation and support of a Master's program in human rights. It shows the need for, and the benefits of, such components as interdisciplinary studies, space for independent research and discussion, an educational methodology that incorporates both theory and practice, the support of a major university and outreach to all sectors of the national community, with, as the primary target, those professionals who daily work touches on human rights concerns. In practice the program has also benefitted from close relationships with Peruvian civil society, monitoring and collaborating in the work of its graduates, from the introduction of distance/virtual learning to reach human rights and other professionals in the underserved regions of the country, and from encouraging both active students and graduates to disseminate this knowledge in their local communities. IDEH is committed to reinforcing all these dimensions. The program's research confirms their value and recommends them to others seeking to develop similar programs.

Notes

1 See la CVR, Final Report www.cverdad.org.pe.
2 See IDEHPUCP website: www.pucp.edu.pe/IDEHPUCP/index.php?option=com_content&view=article&id=65&Itemid=139.
3 Interview conducted by Salmón (May 19, 2010).
4 Entrevista realizada a Fidel Tubino, profesor de la Maestría en Derechos Humanos, el miércoles 26 de mayo de 2010, con motivo de la presente investigación.
5 Research on human rights education in a post-conflict country published by PUCP and available to students includes "*Los Caminos de la Justicia Penal y los Derechos Humanos*", "*Para cruzar el umbral. Acciones y reflexiones para la construcción de la paz y la democracia en el Perú 2005–2006*", "*Miradas que construyen: Perspectivas multidisciplinarias sobre los derechos humanos*" and "*Los sitios de la memoria. Procesos sociales de la conmemoración en el Perú.*"
6 MA outreach: With these considerations in mind, IDEH and the Raoul Wallenberg Institute of Sweden, with financial support from the Swedish Agency for International

Development (SIDA) created the *Specialized Program on Women's Human Rights*. Its objective is to provide academic training, capacity-building, and support in project development for professionals and institutions or organizations that work on women's human rights in the Latin American region. To improve women's rights in the Latin American region, the program set two specific objectives: (1) capacity-building in the promotion and defense of women's human rights for representatives of public and private institutions that work on women's human rights especially among economically disadvantaged and indigenous women, and (2) the formation of the intellectual skills needed to use a gender perspective to diagnose the work of the institution that he/she belongs to. This program held two training sessions in 2008: one in Lund, Sweden and the second, in Lima and Cusco. The program attracted 25 participants from 13 Latin American countries, in addition to the national and foreign experts on women's human rights. The success of the program has set in motion plans for another which will use the distance learning and virtual techniques tested in the Master's program to prepare participants prior to their meeting on site. This program is still being planned. It is seen as of major importance on account of the extent of the violence and other human rights abuses that women in Peru face on a daily basis.

6 Addressing the causes of conflict
Human rights education in Liberia

The conflict in Liberia

Beginning in the 1970's and continuing into the first decade of the twenty-first century, the nation of Liberia was plunged into a series of alternating civil wars and dictatorships. Hundreds of thousands of Liberians were killed and many thousands of others tortured and the festering violence and ethnic animosity linger on to this day. Under the regime of Samuel K. Doe, who seized power and became president via a military coup staged in 1980, ethnic tensions reached boiling-point, as members of the Mano and Gio ethnic groups were targeted by Doe and his administration. Atrocities reported from this period include extrajudicial executions, unlawful killings, illegal or prolonged detentions without trial, and the torture of opposition leaders.[1] A rebel insurgency, ignited by Charles Taylor's National Patriotic Front of Liberia (NPFL) and supported by seven different warring factions, managed to topple Doe in December of 1990.

Over the next 15 years Liberia was plunged into a maelstrom of economic and social chaos. During this time more than 270,000 people were killed and millions were displaced both internally and externally. The net result was the destruction of the economy and hence pervasive hopelessness for ordinary citizens. Only those associated with the timber, rubber, and diamond industries had a relatively secure livelihood. Outside the main towns social services ceased to function, and few school buildings were left standing. The limited amount of primary and secondary education still available was dispensed by a few local teachers willing to work for little or no pay. The situation was, and still is, aggravated by seepage across Liberia's borders of bands of mercenaries and individuals fleeing from, and at other times to, neighboring countries also suffering from civil unrest, notably Sierra Leone, Guinea, and the Ivory Coast.

The fighting continued until 1997, when Charles Taylor, the man most responsible for destabilizing the country, was elected almost unanimously to the presidency. Everyone hoped there would be peace at last, and a UN peacebuilding office was set up in Monrovia. Much of the substance of the 1995 Abuja Accord was ignored, however, notably the proposed reforms of the army and police and the creation of a national human rights commission (Sesay 1996). By

1999 fighting had resumed between Liberians United for Reconciliation and Democracy (LURD) and Charles Taylor's government.

During the civil war gross human rights abuses were committed by all the armed factions. Those violations included summary executions and arbitrary arrests, detentions, tortures, and other forms of ill-treatment; rape and sexual violence; attacks on members of the human rights community; recruitment of child soldiers; and sexual slavery. In 2003, the parties to Liberia's Comprehensive Peace Agreement (CPA)—agreed to in Accra by the then government and the major Liberian rebel groups and politicians—committed themselves to ensuring the prompt and efficient implementation of a broad range of programs designed to foster national healing: cantonment; disarmament; demobilization; rehabilitation and reintegration; disbandment of irregular forces; holding of parliamentary and presidential elections; reforming and restructuring of the Liberian Armed Forces; restructuring of the National Police Force, the Immigration Force, Special Security Service, customs officials and other such statutory security units.[2]

The CPA agreement eventually led to the election in 2005 of Ellen Johnson Sirleaf as president. Her administration struggled with the daunting task of national reconstruction, especially the delivery of basic services, in the face of the high expectations of war-weary Liberians.[3] Over 60 percent of the country's population lives below the poverty line, with most citizens living on less than a dollar a day. Other problems were and continue to be: high levels of illiteracy and unemployment; a shortage of trained and qualified workers; severe destruction and lack of basic infrastructure with respect to electricity, potable water, road networks, health and educational facilities, courthouses, police stations, and correctional facilities; the obliteration of many livelihoods, especially in the agricultural sector; and the destruction of family and community structures. The situation has been even worse in the rural communities where the destruction of houses and community services by the warring factions has been most rampant.

Introducing human rights education

The extraordinary devastation described above is the context for Liberian HRE efforts. Ellen Johnson Sirleaf's government has called for human rights education to be incorporated into the curricula of all the nation's primary, secondary, and tertiary schools; but the actual implementation of such an agenda has not yet begun. The UN Human Rights Council's Working Group on the Universal Peer Review of Liberia[4] points to three obstacles to human rights education in Liberia: the lack of any human rights awareness among large segments of the society; delays in the domestic dissemination and enforcement of the major regional and international human rights conventions; and inadequate financial resources to implement HRE projects.[5] The national school system is widely seen as being the channel for teaching human rights. Indeed, the Liberian government has designed and proclaimed a Peace, Human Rights and Citizenship Education (PEHCED) program for use in the elementary and secondary schools, and has provided some in-service training for teachers. The problem is that the education system is still struggling to rebuild the 90 percent of educational facilities destroyed in the civil wars and to ensure that teachers are paid regularly, a salary of $50 US a month.

Human rights education may be valued by the educational authorities, but the overall education system is not yet ready to promote it, let alone set up the needed teacher training. All of which means that as of now, HRE remains in the hands of a few local NGOs and their international supporters. And given the fact that only a few NGOs are able to mobilize the resources to promote HRE systematically, its overall social impact is limited. Moreover, even educated citizens tend to treat the subject with indifference in their daily lives, although they would not deny outright its relevance to Liberian society as a whole. NGO leaders recognize that virtually all educated Liberians believe in the rule of law as the chief protector of their rights and those of all citizens (Yarsiah 2010). Those same Liberians, however, are not yet committed to ensuring that the national education system becomes a tool used to educate Liberians in citizenship and human rights. This lack of commitment is reflected in the overall operation of government. Government officials see the promotion of human rights knowledge as a double-edged sword. In their public statements they favor the promotion of human rights and bringing policies into compliance with international standards. In practice they often show little respect for citizens who advocate for human rights. This is not surprising given that advocacy invariably highlights human rights abuses and malfeasance on the part of the officials themselves.

The work of the Rights and Rice Foundation in the Foya District of Liberia

The Rights and Rice Foundation (RRF) is a non-governmental organization founded in 2005 and registered in Liberia. Its overall aim is working for social justice and community empowerment. Located in Monrovia, the capital of Liberia, it is especially dedicated to (a) peacebuilding, and human rights and democracy promotion and (b) literacy, numeracy, life-skills, and participatory community-development training and practices. The vision of RRF is, "An equitable society characterized by respect for the rule of law and equal opportunities for all." The mission statement is: "To promote social, economic and political rights through empowering people who suffer injustice and lack equal opportunities."

Their program in the Foya District was aimed at communities in one district, strategically located between two other neighboring countries, Guinea and Sierra Leone in the Mano River Sub region. The Foya District is located in Lofa County, a rural region in the north of Liberia that is home to several ethnic groups, in particular the Muslim Mandingo and the largely Christian Loma. During the civil war, Lofa County was rife with struggles between the Mandingo and the Loma. Not only was this region used as a base by the insurgent forces opposing Charles Taylor's NPFL, but from 1991 to 1996, Mandingo forces and

Loma forces (ULIMO-K and the Lofa Defense Force, respectively) also tried to make it their base. Repeated raids and much back-and-forth action continued throughout the 1990s into the 2000s, creating turmoil, and resulting in vast civilian displacements and inflicting physical and psychological damage upon communities. As in other parts of Liberia during the civil war and within the context of ethnic struggles, young people in Lofa County were targeted for recruitment into the various ethnically-based forces almost as soon as they could carry a gun.[6]

Although the armed conflict has officially ended, conflict and communal violence coupled with the lack of justice mechanisms remain all too typical in many of the Lofa County communities where the Rights and Rice Foundation works. Lacking access to resources, people often resort to coercion and conflict, as opposed to buying and trading to satisfy their basic needs. Conflicts between neighbors or communities often erupt over scarce land, crops, livestock, and water resources. When people, and especially women, go to judges to seek redress, they rarely receive a fair hearing. Corruption has been and remains rampant, and as a result, judges do not arbitrate cases fairly. Plaintiffs then give up, because it costs too much to go on. Without the committed support of their supervisors, the local police, when they exist at all, are unwilling or unable to enforce the laws. Children in these communities are especially vulnerable, as often they are treated as a source of free labor.

In the Foya District within Lofa County the Rights and Rice Foundation implements its Peacebuilding and Reconciliation Project (PRP), the main goal of which is to help communities rebuild themselves around human rights frameworks designed to bring about reconciliation and peace. In a telephone interview James Yarsiah, the Foundation's director, outlined the basic approach of the RRF as follows:

> In order for there to be lasting peace in our country we must address the root causes of the Liberian conflict. It should come as no surprise that we have incorporated an in-depth analysis of these reasons into the HRE program. And since no such cause runs deeper than the violations of the rights of the ordinary people that were perpetrated by the former rulers of Liberia, we must ensure that Liberia's people not only are aware of their rights but know how to go about defending and protecting them. Above all we must believe that major advances in conflict prevention and resolution will come about only when the rights of people are respected, under a governance system that upholds the rule of law.

To ensure that the rights of people are respected, the people have to know that they have rights, including the right to learn what those rights are. Education about rights is one means to protect them and to prevent their violation. However, educators from RRF believe that it is not sufficient to talk about rights; rather, the talk of human rights must be accompanied by advocacy and work toward social change.

This commitment to action-learning and broad-based advocacy has led to perhaps the major accomplishment of the Rights and Rice Foundation to date, namely its establishment of Community Peace Committees (CPCs) in several communities in the Foya District. Each committee is composed of nine members chosen to reflect proportionately the overall population, and thus typically includes women, men, elders, and young people. The primary function of these entities is to adjudicate the local, non-criminal conflicts that arise, but they also spread awareness of human rights principles and practices as delineated in international and domestic law. Through a combination of these educational and other advocacy activities, the RRF educators are helping Liberia's local communities to become more self-reliant and more peaceful places in which to live.

The Human Rights Education Program

The work of the Rights and Rice Foundation on this project began in 2007 when it received a grant from the German Agency for Technical Cooperation to implement HRE training designed to upgrade the human rights, conflict prevention, and mediation knowledge and skills of the CPCs. Each of the training workshops, held in ten communities where the CPCs were already operating, lasted about a week. A follow-up to the training was a program of mentoring and coaching for the CPC leaders by RRF educators. This happened generally in the form of visits paid to the homes of CPC members over the ensuing weeks.

The Rice and Rights Foundation designed a HRE curriculum to be used as the principal means of training these community leaders. It builds upon the Universal Declaration of Human Rights (UDHR) as well as elements of the Liberian Constitution (1986 version), and the Inheritance Law and the Anti-Rape Law as they pertain to women.[7] In addition to giving information about human rights, civil rights, and the Inheritance and Anti-Rape Laws, other lessons involve discussing the causes of the Liberian conflict and the reasons for its extreme violence, the processes of peacebuilding, and the functions of the CPCs. The overall goal is to build up the capacity of the CPC learners with respect to human rights pedagogy and content by presenting those in ways that make sense to ordinary Liberians. The CPC learners are considered "multipliers" because they are expected to spread the learning methods and content associated with their training to other CPC members and to the community at large.

RRF has adopted participatory approaches including the DELTA method, Development and Leadership Training in Action,[8] a training approach centered on the teaching of the renowned Brazilian educator Paulo Freire. The teaching method adopted was participatory learning, in which the trainers from RRF serve as facilitators, helping learners to discover what they already know and guiding them, through dialogue and critical thinking in the acquisition of new ideas on the various topics. The approach employs a method of self-discovery in which participants are presented with graphics, songs, and role-play as ways to analyze the problems and other issues they face in their communities. By analyzing the graphically presented problems, the participants are encouraged to discover for themselves some of the solutions to them, and to devise strategies for implementing the solutions that they themselves have outlined. They are encouraged to use these same strategies when they return to their communities to train others.

The interpretation and translation of the UDHR into the language and daily experience of the participants is the core methodology of their HR capacity-building. RRF educators simplify the UDHR's language and make concrete clarifications with respect to both content and format in ways that correspond to people's daily behavior.[9] Typically each of the rights is translated into ideas that community members feel will resonate widely. Given the importance of duties and responsibilities in human rights practice in African nations, the related responsibilities are taught alongside the rights. In traditional African communities, rights are defined by specific duties, social roles, hierarchies and a person's relationships to the "other" in question. Thus social duties and community responsibilities are implicit in the definition and practice in most African, as well as some societies elsewhere in the world. The related responsibilities and duties are typically taught in tandem with rights. This traditional practice was enshrined in the 1981 African Charter on Human and People's Rights adopted by the Organization of African States, now the African Union. This emphasis is reflected, for example, in the three articles, 27, 28 and 29 of the African Charter that define the duties of the individual with respect to family and society, defined as the nation, the promotion of African unity and the international community at large.

One of the major tensions emerging today is that associated with deeply embedded patriarchal visions of society that often subject women and children to highly subservient roles. The forms of patriarchy vary across different cultures and societies but the outcomes are similar. To be effective the local human rights educators must take into consideration both the traditional definitions and the changes that are now taking place. The particular impact of patriarchy is especially challenging in communities where, as seen in most of the cases in this volume, women have begun to take on increased personal responsibility with respect to peace building and the prevention of violence. In their work the educators must reconcile the new values and human rights standards with the particular roles, responsibilities and culture of their target audience, and make the case for the validity of the resulting social changes. Thus local educators especially understand and explain the role that taking personal responsibility plays in the context of peacebuilding. They must transpose the new values and rights into particular roles and responsibilities and make the case for the validity of the change. The list of rights and responsibilities on the next page (Table A) is used by RRF educators

Above all else, the RRF human rights educators underscore the need to address the root causes of a conflict. They firmly believe that they can change people's behavior only by promoting a new set of rules and expectations that encourages people to act peacefully toward one another. The aforementioned list of rights and responsibilities helps them to do that. At the core of all their educational work is the participatory process: engaging learners in defining the rights and responsibilities that are most relevant to their situations, and finding ways to incorporate a sense of rights and responsibilities into their conflict prevention and resolution efforts.

Table A

Rights	Responsibilities
We are all born free and equal.	Respect and don't violate the freedoms of others.
Don't discriminate.	Accept and see all humans as one, no matter your age, color, sex, nationality, tribe, and origin.
Respect everyone's right to life.	Value, protect, and respect your life, and the lives of others.
Everyone should have a decent salary, with no past or present forced labor	We should not make anyone a slave or force them to work, but we should work toward the development, greater welfare, and improvement of our community and country.
There must be no torture	Do not to harm, hit, or bully others.
We all have the same right to invoke the law	Know and respect the law.
We all are protected by the law.	Do not commit crimes and break the law.
Fair treatment by fair courts	Accept what the law says, but speak up when you feel that a legal judgment has been unfair.
No unfair detainment	Thoroughly investigate before putting someone in prison.
The right to trial	Take disputes to court, where the law decides.
Innocent until proven guilty	Find out the truth, and don't be swayed by rumors.
Everyone has the right of privacy	Mind your own business; don't spoil people's good names, go into their homes, open their letters, or bother them.
Freedom of movement	Don't settle in unlawful places.
Right to asylum	Follow the legal procedures for traveling.
Right to a nationality	As a citizen, respect the laws of your country.
Marriage and family	Seek to fulfill all of your family's needs.
Freedom of thought	Listen to others, respect or at least tolerate their views.
Freedom of speech	You will be held responsible for any actions that ensue from your words, be they good or bad.
Freedom of assembly	Discuss all matters calmly, and take full responsibility for the outcome of the meeting.
Democracy	Follow electoral processes, to vote and to be voted for.
Social security	Pay your taxes to the national government.
Worker's rights	Learn, and make yourself marketable.
Right to play	Know when and how to play; involve others; respect game rules.
A bed, and some food	Work hard, to feed yourself and your family.
Education	Study hard, and abide by all rules and regulations.
Culture and copyright	Respect the rules and norms of the culture; seek permission from authors before making copies of others' writings.
A fair and free world	Behave in an orderly manner, respecting and protecting the welfare of everyone in the society.
Nobody can take away these rights	Observe and respect other people's rights.
	We have a duty to other people, above all a duty to respect their rights and their freedoms.

Assessing human rights education's impact

To better understand the impact of the CPCs, in March of 2010 a Liberian researcher affiliated with RRF visited three communities where the CPCs were working and conducted focus groups with community members.[10] In general the feedback received was positive. The CPCs have helped to foster in the local communities a greater sense of self-reliance and self-determination, and a source of empowerment not only for individuals but for entire communities. More specifically, the focus groups, by pointing to several specific impacts, showed that the CPCs are beginning to address problems and produce small improvements in everyday life.

First, the new ability to turn to a local source for help in resolving a conflict, as the people have been able to do with the CPCs, has helped people to find redress from a competent non-corrupt authority. This is a change from the past. During the civil conflicts and well into the post-conflict period government officials were largely absent, corrupt, or incompetent. This meant that ordinary citizens had to act as their own agents if they wanted to solve their problems, using whatever means, legal or otherwise, were at hand. For example some community leaders would act as judges, adjudicating cases and imposing illegal fines—which they pocketed.

Not only was it costly and indeed, for many, prohibitive to pursue such trials, but various rights of women and children, such as inheritance rights, were often violated because the victims lacked any awareness of their legal rights and thus all too readily abided by the rulings of these courts. Even when they did possess such knowledge they were afraid to go against the ruling of a community leader, for fear of possible fierce reprisals. Women now willingly go to the CPCs to have their complaints heard. The prompt conflict management brought them savings in time and money. Additionally, the labor and resources previously expended upon settling minor conflicts are now being devoted to upgrading families' livelihoods and to community initiatives.

As for community initiatives, the CPCs have helped to resolve the conflicts that have arisen among participants in community-development projects. Now, when disputes arise in the course of a group project, those involved know they can get help from the CPC. Thus a conflict that otherwise might have grown in scope tends to be addressed early on and work on the project at hand does not come to a complete stop. A good example in this regard is a school-building project that was halted when a conflict broke out among the volunteers because some thought that the school should not be built. Here's how one participant attests to the effectiveness in this case:

> It helps us, especially in that we organize ourselves to make projects, and within this project we understand ourselves and bring peace amongst ourselves. Even in the group work, we do group work that can help us to bring peace among ourselves. So these are the changes, and before what used to happen is we would work individually but now we have come together

making food, making projects for ourselves. So that we can develop our town with projects. We have the town school as a project, we have done that and it has benefited us. There was a small conflict during the project but we could resolve it with the guidance of the CPC. This helps not only us but our children, because they go to school and it is their right for them to go to school. This time you can tell your friend that his children should go to school. All the children here now go to school.

The source of many conflicts between communities is almost always the availability of scarce resources in the community; for example, a community may have no access to a water supply and thus must go to a neighboring community for water. This problem often arises when a neighboring community, zealously guarding its water supply, shuts down the pump, thereby creating conflict between the two groups. These conflicts are often exacerbated because they fall along ethnic lines, especially inflammatory being the conflict between the Mandingo and Loma groups in the Foya District and other parts of Lofa County during and after the civil war, as noted earlier in this chapter. The local CPCs have drawn upon both their knowledge of human rights and their conflict-resolution skills in order to resolve such disputes between different communities.

Through the HRE programs the CPCs were able to raise awareness and tackle specific human rights issues where there was a serious lack of knowledge. They, the CPCs, are ensuring that that the local authorities know about not only human rights in the abstract, but also in relation to their presence within national law. This process has been especially vital in connection with educating local authorities about the rights of women and children. With respect to the former, numerous local male leaders give voice to their new realization that women have specific rights guaranteed under Liberia's Inheritance Law and have heard the women themselves reporting that men now are less likely to violate their rights.

Since 2007, RRF field-program organizers have witnessed a major increase in the participation of women, both in attendance at the training programs and in their active involvement in community meetings and decision-making. When the RRF project was initiated in the Foya District, women's participation was at a low ebb; they could be found sitting outside meeting halls, or when women did enter the halls, they said nothing because their husbands insisted on talking on their behalf. Given this and other ways in which men suppress women, there were many, mostly covert, marital conflicts. But now, when and if such conflicts arise, more women are willing to turn to the CPCs, who will intervene to sort out the situation.

The HRE programs that focus on children's rights have become particularly popular. They are designed to make parents aware of the fact that children are rights-bearers. Parents have begun to realize that their children are not mere tools to be used to work out their own anger and frustrations, but rather are to be treated as human beings who possess the right to seek their own happiness. Children's rights educators have addressed the particular problem of corporal punishment, a major issue in a society where it has long been the correction method used to discipline children, especially in rural areas. Beating children has traditionally been seen not as a negative act, but rather a correctional step, taken to scare them away from repeating a transgression. Through HRE programs parents are taught that not much is learned through physical punishment and that real discipline entails respecting children, appreciating that they will make their own mistakes no matter what. Comments such as the following reveal how consciousness has been raised, and actions altered, as a direct result of many Liberians' new awareness of the rights of women as well as children.

> Even wife-beating—it was a little rampant, but since the training it has been minimized. Even to beat our children that way is not correct. They used to beat the child on a whim, like it was a dog, and now they minimize it. It was happening here, it was happening readily, it was happening here. Beating our children, wife, our lover … it was not good, but the HRE training reduced it.
>
> There is a big change because today they [the local chiefs] allow women to be in their midst. When they are talking, women also participate in the talking. Even children can speak; they have the right to participate in the talking.

There also has been a significant shift in attitudes when it comes to parents' old practice of making their children tend their farms and do other work before attending school. Parents who have become aware of their children's rights are beginning to encourage them to prioritize, and continue with their schooling. Such trends have led to an increase in primary school enrollment and attendance in those communities where the CPCs are operative. Thanks to ongoing HRE efforts the children and youth are increasingly becoming aware of their rights, including their right to an education. Thus at home, adults and children are engaging in dialogues about education as a right, and working together on ensuring that kids receive an education. A trend is emerging: the greater the community members' awareness of human rights, the more fearful they are of doing anything that might be seen as constituting a violation. This new, and still hugely fragile ethos is one that benefits women and children especially.

It is also important to mention that children and youth are expected and trained to serve on the CPCs. Their particular task is to target other young people with human rights messages, and thereby avert or at least soften the conflicts that inevitably arise among young people and so give them a role in the community. The CPCs have begun to create small-group activities, designed to teach young people new tools of expression as well as their rights and responsibilities. In some places the youth have taken on projects that address their basic needs more directly, but much more remains to be done.[11] By broadly disseminating an awareness of human rights, the CPCs are helping to reintegrate young people into the social and political life of the community in an effort to facilitate the healing process and to forestall further conflict. A young participant in an HRE program said this: "By knowing your rights, and then you respect other people's rights. So in that regard you are preventing conflict."

Challenges

Since 2006 the CPCs have grown in both their status and acceptance in the communities, and in the effectiveness of their work. In the early years the CPCs were not well received. An evaluation conducted in 2007 cites that resistance to them was common.[12] It notes that the committees were not always supported by the local authorities for multiple reasons, not least because the committees were viewed as taking lucrative cases away from them. Interviews conducted by Patience Lardner in 2010, however, began to paint a different picture. There was evidence of a greater than expected acceptance of the role the CPC plays in the various communities. Part of the acceptance springs from the fact that the committees have upgraded their capacity to deal with conflicts, and as a result they are seen as fostering greater social stability and more harmonious social relations within the communities where they operate.

On a more practical level, community residents have begun to see the economic and political benefits that human rights education and practices add to life, in part by enhancing the various forms of human capital. Even more important, however, for people living in absolute poverty, is the new, direct connection they are making between human rights awareness and a lesser need for the intervention of government officials outside the community. Homegrown conflict-resolution means savings that accrue to individuals in the form of both time and money. Finally, as more and more people equate the improved local conflict-resolution mechanisms with economic benefits, they become that much more motivated to make human rights learning a permanent aspect of their communities.

In summary, human rights education and the outreach programs of the CPC have served to: help Liberians resolve their interpersonal conflicts peacefully; save money; increase the participation of women and children in decision-making; reduce the rights violations against women and children; and upgrade the capacity of communities for self-governance and thereby for self sufficiency. The two chief target groups (women and young people) are beginning to emerge as agents capable of bringing change and peace to their communities (Yarsiah 2010). The HRE activities of the CPC have been shown to nurture these positive developments.

However, the CPCs are in a certain sense the victim of their own success, for people in the Foya District are now adherents of HRE programs, and are much more aware of the wide extent of their own needs, such that they are demanding much more of the CPC people than they are able to accomplish. The following are the words of the translator, conveying the answers given by various participants in the survey to the following question "What are some of the things you think the program should do, to be of more benefit to your community?":

- He is saying that one thing that the program should do for them is to have drinking water. Because they don't have any place to drink.
- He is saying the same thing, that they don't have drinking water. That it is a major problem, and its solution would help lead to peace.

- He says the same thing, that if they had good drinking water they would be healthy and there would be peace.
- We especially want a line of safe drinking water. It will bring peace amongst ourselves, especially between our neighboring communities. We would like a pump.
- He is saying that another thing they lack, they don't have good shelter and another important thing is water.
- He said their problem in the community is the need for a clinic, a (Palaba) peace hut and a sawmill. That if they have this, they can be happy in their community and they will foster peace.
- She said they really need a toilet. They don't have toilets in their community. They go in the bush. Also, they need water. That is what she thinks the program should do for them.
- Okay, I just want to add onto the same thing that was said concerning the school system, the school construction. The building is small so we want an additional annex, to upgrade our schooling.
- We need help for a health post. We don't have a place for childbirth. If we had a health post or a clinic, it would be good for our community.
- We need help from the group to build a Palaba hut for the CPC members, so that we can have a place to hold a meeting and discuss the development of our community.

Those working in the fields of human rights advocacy and education in Liberia know that it is not sufficient just to talk about rights, talk must be accompanied by work that addresses life-needs and leads to social changes. One major concern shared with researchers by the RRF personnel and the CPC members interviewed for this study is the challenge of teaching learners about their human rights when such rights are conspicuous only by their absence from their lives, and even scarcer are the means of redress. RRF human rights educators and members of the CPCs lament their inability to back up their teaching with the logistic and institutional support needed to heighten the security of communities. They argue that many learners who have been exposed to human rights education programs have brushed them off because they had, or appeared to them to have, no direct link to their immediate problems of daily living, especially the economic ones (Yarsiah 2010).

The central challenge, then, and one that many members of the CPCs are now contending with is that of integrating the abstract ideals of human rights and human rights laws into the lives of impoverished community members, even though most of their basic human needs—water, food, medical attention, shelter—are not being met. Most broadly, human rights education is not a stand-alone activity but rather needs to be linked with, and integrated into, the entire gamut of human needs and social services.

The second challenge is how best to convey a full, or at least an adequate understanding of human rights laws and institutions. In the course of eliciting from the community members their evaluation of their participation in HRE workshops run by CPC members and representatives from the RRF, the researchers noted that the benefits of acquiring human rights knowledge or awareness were never mentioned, presumably because they were not remembered by them. Rather, they emphasized the skills they had picked up in the areas of mediation and conflict-resolution. Asked what they had learned about human rights, many of the interviewees referred simply to the fact that now they are living in greater harmony with their neighbors, with less conflict, or at least with conflicts being locally resolved. Asked to give an example of human rights, a participant would say something like, "Human rights means to live together peacefully." One exception to this pattern was a fairly widespread understanding of children's rights. When asked to name a specific children's right, the interviewee commonly would cite a child's right to attend school. Many of the CPC educators themselves often had difficulty distinguishing between universal human rights and civil, i.e. national constitutional, rights. Presumably this more detailed knowledge of human rights will come over time, as HRE workers receive more training.

The third challenge facing not just HRE, but society as a whole is the fact that in Liberia today, over half the population (62.6 percent) is below 20 years of age, and where children of less than ten years account for 41.9 percent of the population.[13] Having been directly recruited into the fighting forces of both sides, all too many young Liberians have gained a first-hand understanding of how violence can become a standard modality of expression. Further, whereas many adults have returned to their families and some to their jobs, many young people who were forced to leave school and family behind during the conflict have returned to their communities and found themselves with nothing to do.[14] The CPC approach is teaching that peaceful relations arise when youth are able to enter into purposeful, mutually beneficial dialogues and enterprises with one another.

Conclusion

How can HRE help to bring peace to Liberia? At the very least it has become clear to the educators working in the Foya District that peace can be achieved only through the effective and sustained management of the conflicts that inevitably erupt over scarce resources and economic insecurity. Conflict management does not and cannot exist in a void. In other words, peaceful political and economic development across all of Liberia's regions will be achieved only when its citizens have become fully aware of, and elicit accountability and effectiveness from their government officials by exercising their political and economic rights and responsibilities in ways that enable them to obtain their basic rights and needs. They need to know their rights and be able to articulate them. All of those elements or factors are still in the nascent stage in the Foya District today. However, it can be said that the CPCs that are now in place in various communities, are providing a solid rationale for human rights education simply by helping to foster these different components of peaceful socio-economic development. Further advocacy and capacity-building work will serve to sustain these preliminary efforts.

Notes

1 From the Truth and Reconciliation Commission (TRC) report for Liberia: www.unhcr.org/refworld/publisher,AMNESTY,,LBR,451798cb4,0.html.
2 Liberia: Comprehensive peace agreement between the government of Liberia and the Liberians United for Reconciliation and Democracy (LURD) and the Movement for Democracy in Liberia (MODEL) (2003). usip.org/fifiles/fifile/resources/collections/peace_agreements/liberia_08182003.pdf.
3 During the civil war, for example, the country's ratio of debt to its gross national product (GDP) skyrocketed from 177 to 715 percent. At its level of debt, Liberia was outspending its production by 700 percent. As a measure of the nation's financial difficulties, the ratio both explains the exorbitant amount of borrowing engaged in by the central government in its struggle to meet its expenses, and represents the deplorable state of the country's finances during the period in question. Expectations remain high, but in some quarters hope is beginning to dwindle. The government has implemented debt-reduction programs through participation in the IMF's Heavily Indebted Poor Countries (HIPC) Initiative, as part of its attempt to drastically upgrade the country's economic status.
4 Available at www.ohchr.org/EN/HRBodies/UPR/Pages/LRSession9.aspx.
5 Liberia: National report submitted in accordance with paragraph 15(a) of the annex to Human Rights Council Resolution 5/1*. 2010. Geneva, Switzerland: United Nations General Assembly, A/HRC/WG.6/9/LBR/1 [accessed June 13, 2011], lib.ohchr.org/HRBodies/UPR/.../A_HRC_WG.6_9_LBR_1_Liberia-eng.pdf.
6 www.international-alert.org/sites/default/files/publications/201011IFPIofasecurity.pdf.
7 Taking into account the high incidence of rape against girls and women in post-conflict Liberia, in 2005 the government enacted legislation to amend the new Penal Code of 1976—the Rape Law. In the following year and under the leadership of the Ministry of Gender and Development, a National Gender Based Violence Plan of Action was launched. The main objective of the National Plan is to prevent the high incidence of gender-based violence in different communities and provide physical, psychological, economic and legal support to girls and women victims of gender based violence. *Source: National plan of action for the prevention and management of gender based violence in Liberia.* (2006). Liberia: Gender Based Violence Interagency Taskforce, GBV-POA [accessed June 13, 2011], http://s3.amazonaws.com/dna_futures/original/65/National_Gender-based_Violence_Plan_of_Action.pdf?1352415241.
8 DELTA or the Development Education Leadership Teams in Action, www.crvp.org/book/Series02/II-10/chapter-18.htmwww.crvp.org/book/Series02/II-10/chapter-18.htm.
9 There are 16 major ethnic groups in Liberia: Bassa, Belle, Dahn (Gio), Dei, Gbandi, Gola, Grebo, Kissi, Kpelle, Krahn, Krao (Kru), Lorma, Mandingo, Mahn (Mano), Mende, and Vai. While the official language of Liberia is English most Liberians speak one of the 16 ethnic dialects. *Source: 2010 Human Rights Report: Liberia.* 2011, Bureau of Democracy, Human Rights, and Labor [accessed June 14, 2007], www.state.gov/g/drl/rls/hrrpt/2010/af/154354.htm.
10 The study focused on the ability of communities to handle conflicts as a result of their training in human rights education programs provided by RRF over the past two years. In May 2010 a member of RRF's team, Patience Lardner, traveled to the communities of Kpangbeinin, Senga, Bandeinin, Ngissakonja and Peyama, with an estimated number of inhabitants in each community 150–200. Over the course of five days, she conducted six interviews in each community with CCP and other community members. All the interviewees were residents of the Foya District in the north-western part of Liberia, a location that borders both Sierra Leone, which has itself only recently emerged from an 11-year conflict and Guinea, which is now descending into its own difficult period. All of these interviews were recorded, transcribed, and translated. Interpreters were used in some cases, if the researcher did not know the local

language spoken by the interviewee. She also conducted focus-group interviews in each community with these having been taped but not transcribed. Each of the groups was comprised of from six to eight community members who had been contacted with the help of the CPC members.

11 In addition to questions about human rights education program our research protocol included two additional questions that our participants had raised as concerns and that were foremost in their minds. The questions were as follows: What are some of the things you think the program should do, to make it be of more benefit to your community? Do you have anything else on your mind that you would like us to know?

12 Trentmann, Claudia (January 2008). "Summary Evaluation Report, Support to Reconstruction in West Lofa County, GTZ SRWL (2005–2008), Evaluation of GTZ's Development-oriented Emergency and Transitional Aid project in Liberia using OECD-DAC criteria for evaluating humanitarian action," Foya Liberia.

13 Source: *2010 Human Rights Report: Liberia*, (2011). Bureau of Democracy, Human Rights, and Labor [accessed June 13, 2011], www.state.gov/g/drl/rls/hrrpt/2010/af/154354.html.

14 *Nothing left to lose: The legacy of armed conflict and Liberia's children* (2004). Watchlist: On Children and Armed Conflict [accessed June 10, 2011], www.watchlist.org/reports/pdf/liberia.report.pdf.

7 The City of Women in Cartagena, Colombia, a human rights community of practice

The conflict in Colombia

During the 1990s and into the mid-2000s the conflict in Colombia led to the displacement of tens of thousands of people. Displacement has been used as a weapon in the conflict, yet there is complete impunity for the perpetrators (Ariza *et al.* 2009). Female heads of household who make up 28.1 percent of the national population comprise 46 percent of the displaced. Human Rights Watch (2005) has documented the many deleterious effects of forced displacement, among them alarming rates of post-traumatic stress disorder (PTSD), increased incidences of domestic violence, lack of access to health care and sanitary living conditions, high rates of unemployment, and an under-representation of displaced children in school.

In Colombia thousands of displaced people have filed *acciones de tutela*, legal procedures established by the constitution that have allowed individuals to petition the Constitutional Court directly for protection of their fundamental human rights. Indeed, as of 2003, over 1,000 cases had been filed by displaced persons (Cepeda-Espinosa 2005: 6). After compiling and reviewing 108 of these cases, the Court issued judgment T-025/04 in January 2004[1] which condemned government inaction and even accused government officials of outright discrimination toward displaced persons. Noting that the problem was not attributable to a single authority but rather a systemic structural deficiency, the Court concluded that

> Given the conditions of extreme vulnerability of the displaced population, as well as the repeated omission by the different authorities in charge of their assistance to grant timely and effective protection, the rights of the plaintiffs in the present proceedings—and of the displaced population in general—to a dignified life, personal integrity, equality, petition, work, health, social security, education, minimum subsistence income and special protection for elderly persons, women providers and children, have all been violated [and] have been taking place in a massive, protracted, and reiterative manner.
>
> (Colombian Constitutional Court 2004: 10)

The Court, in issuing its decision, drew on both the 1997 Colombian Law 387 and the UN Guiding Principles on Internal Displacement to declare the current state of affairs unconstitutional and ordered an immediate, sustained, and coordinated national response.

The League of Displaced Women

> Indeed, it is widely acknowledged that in Colombia, the work of defending human rights has become a high-risk activity, and that those organizations that struggle for the restitution of our rights have in many cases been persecuted or threatened. The Liga de Mujeres Desplazadas has been no exception.
>
> (Ariza *et al.* 2009: 7)

Among the organizations working with the Court, and in the spirit of UN Resolution 1325, is the League of Displaced Women ("the League"). Founded in 1998 by the Colombian human rights lawyer, Patricia Guerrero, the League helps displaced women and specifically a group of them who come from Montes de María, a region that was consumed by violence beginning in the mid 1990s. In the wake of their displacement, and living in the shanty towns on the outskirts of the city of Cartagena, the women faced serious and immediate needs: identification papers, homes, employment, education for their children, and above all a sense of renewed security. In many cases the living conditions in these shanty towns were abysmal, with no running water, no bathrooms, and very few with working toilets connected to sewers.

The League works with over 500 displaced women and their families through a combination of legal and political advocacy. The organization sees "struggle" in its mission—as one of "organized and peaceful resistance by women victims for the restoration of their fundamental and constitutional human rights" (Ariza *et al.* 2009: 7). It also seeks to help women to recover from a range of traumas. For example, 86 percent of the members surveyed in 2009 had been victims of sexual violence, while 33 percent had had a close family member, friend, or partner murdered (ibid.).

The League's work is laid out in its Gender Justice Agenda which has three components: the political-organizational, through which the organization forms networks with other local and international agencies to bring attention to forced displacement; the legal-political, through which they plan legal actions to protect their rights as displaced women, especially when it comes to what they perceive as impunity for the armed groups that caused their displacement; and the community-organizational, through which they train themselves and others to work with displaced women, providing psychological counseling and taking testimonials. All three components are rooted in a gender-approach to human rights, and include elements of human rights education.

It is important to note that the League's educational work takes place within a context of ongoing conflict, and not "post-conflict" as many government officials and others would like the world to believe. Though the armed conflict has ended by all official accounts, these women constantly fear for their own, as well as others' safety. The League is perceived by many as posing a threat to the armed groups' control over the communities of Bolívar. Three reasons explain why many of its actions have been seen as threatening by those who control local communities. First, the League has stood up against local corruption and promotes the values of equality, non-discrimination, and non-violence. Second, some of the League's displaced women witnessed crimes perpetrated by paramilitary members who are currently being prosecuted. And third, the paramilitary demobilization is not being properly monitored by the local authorities and is perpetuating these groups' sense of complete impunity. The League's members, and especially its leaders, have openly criticized such impunity, and have received frequent threats to their lives. Between 2008 and 2010 the local Ombudsman Office in Cartagena repeatedly announced that the League was at high risk of targeted violence.

Despite these threats the women of the League have been at the forefront of major campaigns to change laws and ensure the protection of their human rights. The legal strategies also have connections to the security risks faced by the women. Of the threats and crimes committed against the League in the last decade, "there has not been a single criminal investigation, let alone conviction, of the crimes committed toward the more than 100 women who are a part of the [League]" (ibid. 2009: 7). This explains why the Gender Justice Agenda has been expressly designed "[to] confront impunity for the crimes committed against internally displaced women and to discover the truth of what led to their forced displacement and to know who was responsible for it; to determine why the state could not prevent it and if there was collusion with the illegal armed groups" (ibid.: 19).

Combining their political-organizational dimension and their legal-political dimension, the League has coordinated with (or appealed to) national authorities, most notably the Constitutional Court, and seeks to hold perceived perpetrators accountable for their crimes. In addition it has joined numerous international partnerships and has served as consultant and signatory to several declarations— including, most recently, a declaration issued by the Latin American and Caribbean Caucus, commemorating the fifteenth anniversary of the Beijing Women's Conference. And since the League was founded in 1999, the Security Council has unanimously passed UN Resolution 1325 on women, peace, and security, urging the inclusion of women's networks in peacebuilding.

Human rights education is a cross-cutting theme that runs throughout all the work of the League. More to the point, in almost every way in which the League's educators are trained to approach their work with displaced women they use a human rights perspective. They actively seek to introduce and help women to apply human rights laws and principles in their everyday engagement with social and political issues. Moreover, through their participation in several of the legal battles led by Patricia Guerrero, the women in the League have become more fully versed in both Colombian law and in international human rights law.

The City of Women

Despite the overtly hostile environment in which they operate, in 2003, the League undertook the creation of the City of Women (La Ciudad de las Mujeres); a housing project in the municipality of Turbaco (Bolívar), located 20 minutes from downtown Cartagena. The City of Women (which was completed in 2006), supports the notion that basic needs (shelter and income) must be met before women can open themselves up to all their human rights, and to participate in struggles that support the fulfillment of their rights. The importance of meeting the women's basic needs is described on the League's website as follows:

> The houses are small but still feel spacious, with a good living room, two large bedrooms, and a small patio for hanging clothing, in addition to a kitchen and terrace, which some have already made into a nice place to be. The most touching of all is that women talk about this project, which will continue to grow and become more beautiful, with the great pride of those who feel that they not only have a place now to live, but they built it with their sweat and their muscles.
>
> (Liga de Mujeres Desplazadas 2010)

According to a 2007 profile written by the Colombian reporter Cristina Fraga, the idea for the City was to build permanent homes in a self-contained, self-sustaining community for the 300 people who live in the city. To optimize resources and reduce construction costs, the League created a small adobe brick factory which provided work for 30 women, enabling them to use two machines to make the 95,000 adobe cement blocks that were needed for construction. Many of its present day residents were actively involved in this project that led to the construction of 97 homes.

The significance of establishing a self-contained *physical* community of displaced women is both tangible as well as metaphorical. For once, women who have been victimized both in their family life as well as by paramilitary forces and drug traffickers were able to collaborate, building homes for themselves and one another, even while learning about and striving to protect their human rights. By building and maintaining the City themselves, the women asserted authority over their own lives, collaborating with one another in pursuit of a larger goal. The process of erecting homes became a cathartic experience, filled with on-the-ground learning about human rights through individual introspection as well as group conversations and meetings.

Unfortunately, the City of Women has not yet eluded the violence that its inhabitants thought they had left behind. During the three-year period that the City was being constructed, messages from the past kept appearing, often of the worst kind: "[D]eath squads began to leave dismembered dead bodies next to the development site or in the corn fields which served as the source of livelihood for many women and children" (Fraga 2007). And for those who have belonged to the League since 1999 (seven years prior to the opening of the City of

Women) there have been two assassinations, one attempted murder, five rapes, one forced disappearance, and multiple threats to the leaders. For this reason the City of Women is guarded by two former army officers and its leaders are encouraged not to travel alone. Still, despite international attention and higher levels of protection, in January 2007 the City of Women's community center was burned down, apparently in an arson attack staged by a paramilitary group.

Despite these many challenges, however, the City of Women has continued to expand. In addition to the homes, they have built a multi-service center where women can acquire skills through training sessions. Some women are now being trained as bricklayers and others to work in agriculture. All of them receive training in women's rights, national and international law, leadership and advocacy skills. The women articulate human rights laws and principles with astonishing acumen and expertise. For their children too, there have been benefits. The multi-service center also serves the 300 schoolchildren who are the sons and daughters of many of these women. Meanwhile the League members are carrying out new phases of building construction. To help fortify their knowledge about human rights and strengthen their advocacy and organizational skills, the League sends teams of women to the City training in gender, human rights, and participatory social research. The latter includes the recording of testimonials. According to League educators, one of the hardest elements in their work with women involves the taking of testimonials from those who have been victims of egregious human rights violations in the past. While they are careful to avoid re-victimizing these women—something that could occur if the women are forced to relive past traumatic events as they retell them—the League's staff members insist that knowledge of these stories is vital because they reveal the violence women in Colombia have suffered. The struggle to make the needs of women visible—and to hold accountable those who were responsible for their displacement—has continued to be one of the most important tasks for the organization, "not only for those who have decided to give their testimony and denounce what happened to them, but also for the women who continue to have their voices silenced, victims of fear and ignorance" (Ariza *et al.* 2009: 21).

HRE workshops led in part by lawyers "explain [to the women] the origin of the violations, their consequences, and the imperative [to act]" (ibid.: 8). Patricia Guerrero explains that human rights education begins with women gathering to analyze their problems. Discussions focused on understanding the gender gap, the rights of women, and the distortions produced by a history of discrimination, and above all the importance of women as key players in rebuilding the social fabric that is continually being frayed by the violence and crime brought on by forced displacement. The League's HRE workshops demonstrate how women can look for opportunities to engage in deliberation that can lead to the recognition of unmet needs and unrecognized rights, and to the development of strategies for change.

It should be noted that taking women's testimonials is a vital part of the human rights education process associated with the League's work. Through the process of developing these written testimonials and discussing their experiences with others the women acquired a deeper knowledge about their own experiences. Their participation in the League's work allows women who once were victimized to obtain the information that enables them to recognize that they have human rights which have been violated, to rename their experiences in terms of those rights, and to use their raised awareness to fight back against their oppressors.

Findings: empowerment and human rights education as an act of resistance

> Catarina's right to personal dignity was played out every day, even though it was not highly publicized. Carrying around the picture of her sewage-infested home and acknowledging of how far she had come was an illustration of how rights are regained and practiced on a day-by-day basis.[2]

Through their participation in the League's work and its discussion groups these women have become aware of the injustices that have surrounded and permeated their lives. The impact of the League's work on women's empowerment has been profound. Several women acknowledged in their interviews with Paula Ramírez, a researcher who visited the City of Women in 2010,[3] that as displaced women they knew they had some rights, but as human beings they felt, partly owing to the adverse circumstances in the region and communities where they live, that the violation of those rights had become endemic to their everyday life. Moreover, reflections such as these on human rights and gender have laid down the structural base of the organization itself. Interestingly, the organization has developed through the women's experiences feeding directly into it.

All five of the women eloquently testified, in the course of their interviews, to the transformative effect that their participation in the program has had upon them. Deyanira, a seven-year participant in the League, spoke about personal empowerment:

> I started to learn about so many things that I was entitled to and that I could do, and that as a displaced person and as a woman had been taken away from me. We are all entitled to our rights, to justice, and to reparations, and when one begins to recognize all those things to which one has a right, one is motivated to have these rights recognized that as a displaced person were taken away and in that way to start regaining that part of one's life, that stability when one is so very unstable, and to recover that empowerment and respect for these women who have earned it.

In her interview, Marlene expressed her feelings about empowerment through the League in this way:

> After our training is when I started to like the idea of leadership. During our workshops, Doris would say, "Let's do this, who wants to help coordinate

this?" and I lifted a hand and that's when I think I started to connect with the process.

Human rights education has helped women to connect to national and personal reconstruction by giving them a language they can use to redress the wrongs and injustices that hamper them from fulfilling their aspirations. Laura recalled that when she first arrived at the League:

> I didn't even have the right to declare displacement, because I didn't even know what displacement was. I came here through Doris and the team. They helped me and explained to me that I was displaced, and then I began to know about ... my rights and what I could do, and the things I could access. As a woman I had things taken away from me and I had the right to claim them and to be recognized. And we, all of us, have also the right to truth and reparations.

The women acquired initially a dual perspective, namely as people who needed help, and as people who had been helped. This has effectively turned them into people who help others, with such transformations being something that other human rights experts or policy-makers often are unable to foster, regardless of how well versed they may be in the technical details of treaties and legal mandates. Laura, one of the five women interviewed for this study, corroborated this observation, and explained to us how both the organization itself and the ongoing process of struggling for their rights are intimately linked to the reciprocal relationships among the women:

> When you become a leader, you begin to understand that the goals you set for yourself can be even higher. Then it was not only to have my rights recognized and those things, but that I could help others as they were helping me. Having the capacity to help those women who joined us later, and being able to see them through the process of learning about their rights.

Another participant, Sandra, told us how her training in the League has helped her to say "no" but even more important to her was her ability to share this with other women. For her, saying "no" to certain injustices or speaking out for certain entitlements means her own and others' "empowerment". To be able to empower others is one of the hallmarks of the women of the League.

> It's as if a little worm wakes up in you, and you see that you are entitled to something else. Every day you feel like you're learning something that you didn't know, and now I feel like I have the ability to say "no." So I'm starting this process and following through by tolerating more and more voices at the same time, and I have the ability to give this to other women.

Deyanira also expresses this feeling of empowerment and eagerness to share with others her knowledge:

I've been trained and I have become the first field professional. I feel very empowered, and I feel that what I know now, I can pass on to other women but not only to women, also to men who can acquire this knowledge that I am committed to now, and that we can transmit it to others.

Impact assessment: the City of Women as a human rights community of practice

The experience of the League and the City of Women teaches us that we should avoid taking too narrow a view of human rights education. Human rights education encompasses both the explicit teaching of human rights in more formal learning settings (such as in classrooms and the discussion groups) and the more tacit understandings of human rights that are learned from daily living and active participation in meetings and other activities such as those that are part of running the City of Women. Overall, the impact of such experiences on the approximately 300 people living in the City for the past several years has been profound, with many of the older members having moved from a status of novice to advanced human rights practitioners, with a high regard and motivation for improving the overall human rights situation of all displaced women.

The League and the City embody the characteristics of the process that learning theorists call a community of practice. There are three identifiable characteristics of a community of practice (McDermott *et al.* 2002: 163–164), and they are found in the League's women: First, members are bound together by their collectively developed understanding of what their community is about, to the extent that they hold each other accountable to this sense of joint enterprise. To be competent is to understand the enterprise well enough to be able to contribute to it. Second, members build their community through mutual engagement. They interact with one another, establishing norms and relationships of mutuality that reflect these interactions. To be competent is to be able to engage with the community and be trusted as a partner in these interactions. Third, communities of practice produce a shared repertoire of communal resources—language, routines, sensibilities, artifacts, tools, stories, and styles. To be competent is to have access to this repertoire and be able to use it appropriately.

The basic argument made by Jean Lave and Etienne Wenger (1991), is that communities of practice are everywhere and that generally we are involved in a number of them, whether at work, school, home, or in our civic and leisure interests. Wenger (1998), the author of this concept, has put it this way:

> Communities of practice are formed by people who engage in a process of collective learning in a shared domain of human endeavor: a tribe learning to survive, a band of artists seeking new forms of expression, a group of engineers working on similar problems, a clique of pupils defining their identity in the school, a network of surgeons exploring novel techniques, a gathering of first-time managers helping each other cope.

Communities of practice are groups of people who share a concern or a passion for something they do and learn how to do it better as they interact regularly. The League clearly conforms to a community of practice, women inhabiting a shared space for reflection and action in human rights, a place in which they recover from violence. The members are women bound together as a way to protect themselves physically and emotionally from the turmoil of displacement. Their group participation comes from their belief in the value of learning about human rights as a way of gaining redress both individually and collectively. If she is truly to belong to the community, each woman must trust and respect those around her. Having a shared narrative helps in this respect; each woman can identify with her neighbor's past life-experience.

By sharing their stories, the women acquire a sense of self-awareness while simultaneously bonding with one another. And precisely because each woman is part of the overall project the relationships they develop are based on respect, comprehension, and empathy. Also vitally important is the fact that the women share a history in many respects. Even if they did not know each other personally before participating in the League and living together in the City of Women, they can relate to each other on a deep level, thereby fostering a highly effective learning (and practicing) community. By frequently engaging in talks and community activities, the process of learning takes place at both individual and communal levels. By working alongside one another to deepen their knowledge and bolster their confidence, the women embody a community of practice.

The League exemplifies a fully functional community of practice that builds upon its members continually growing in knowledge about human rights. Irene simply said: "One simply wants to learn a little bit more, to be more ambitious; one wants to learn more every day about everything." Our broad conclusion is that as they become more competent human rights practitioners they become more involved in the main processes of the particular community. In the language of Lave and Wenger (1991), they move from "legitimate peripheral participation" into full participation. Learning is thus seen not just as the acquisition of knowledge by individuals, but also as a process of social participation. The nature of each situation impacts significantly on the process (ibid.: 37). The key indicator of impact is the heightened participation of women in the process, which comes about as women not only fully participate, but do so with high levels of understanding about human rights.

Implications for human rights education

This study has sought to answer the question of whether participation in the League has been successful in helping women who have experienced human rights violations to reflect upon and to acquire an understanding of their rights. To that question we can answer yes. But many questions that pertain to the workings of the community of practice remain unanswered: How has being an active participant in the practices of this community helped them to construct human rights based identities? In what ways have they become more competent human rights practitioners? What levels and forms of participation have these women acquired through their participation in the League and by living in the City of Women? How have they evolved from a novice to an experienced group of human rights practitioners? What impacts are currently being felt outside the organization? The study of the City of Women has, however, allowed us to see a different and important model of human rights learning. It also raises questions about how human rights knowledge and skills are learned in this model compared to others, and how they are put to use by community members to create meaning in their lives and to advocate for change.

Whatever the answers to these questions may be, the most significant conclusion that can be drawn from the study is that human rights learning resides within relationships among people. It is not necessarily something individuals possess, something that can be found in their heads. In the present case it is the conditions that have brought these women together and that have allowed the various pieces of human rights information to take on a deeper relevance for them. Where there is no relevance to daily life there is little learning, and even less memory of what has been learned. Human rights learning does not reside in individual persons, but rather in the various conversations of which they are a part. The study also serves to point up the intimate connection between knowledge and activity. Learning is an integral aspect of daily living—problem solving and learning from experience. An educator like Patricia Guerrero, who has been instrumental in designing learning experiences for the women of the League, has reflected deeply on what constitutes knowledge and practice, and for her, education is fundamentally informed and committed action.

Future directions

For the women of the League, their participation in its collective life and their engagement with its activities represent a medium through which they learn something new about human rights every day. The present study has sought to shed some light on the nature of human rights learning as it takes place within communities of practice, and on how knowledge about the impact of human rights is generated. The study has succeeded if it has led those working in the field of human rights to think differently about their groups, networks, and associations, and about the work they do and the reasons they have for doing it. And yet in this study we have merely scratched the surface of what it means to live and learn human rights in the City of Women. There is so much more to be learned about the human rights learning and the strength of that learning. We know that HRE programs should begin with a needs-assessment and be oriented toward helping learners solve their human-rights related problems. Thus it would have been helpful if we had studied what problems the women wanted to resolve and those that they have resolved, and how knowledge about human rights has informed their problem-solving capacities. We know that these women are deeply motivated to learn about human rights, in part because they are involved in advocacy movements that link their personal stories to national narratives.

Thus in the future we need to probe even more deeply into their stories, experiences, and motivations to see how all of these have taken on added significance in their newly perceived relation to human rights and to the world in which they live. This study shows how human rights education and its associated practices have helped these women to advocate for themselves by giving them a language and skills that they can use to redress the wrongs and injustices that they see as keeping them from fulfilling their aspirations. Indeed its apparent success calls for replication and testing in other circumstances.

Equally interesting is evaluating the League's sustainability. In principle, building a physical community with all the necessary basic utilities and services and educational activities assures a greater degree of permanence than the typical human rights education or training program. In practice, however, the community has to be maintained in the face of evolving needs and options, raising questions of both economic sustainability and community politics and management. However, it is legitimate to see these as standard growth problems which, given its established communal management and learning practices, the community is prepared to address.

Notes

1 *Colombian Constitutional Court, Decision no. T-025 of 2004, Colombian Constitutional Court, Decision no. T-025 of 2004*, (2004) [accessed June 14, 2007], www.brookings.edu/~/media/.../Colombia/Colombia_T%20025_2004.pdf.
2 Noonan, "Case Study Draft Report on Colombia" (Independent Project at Harvard University, Cambridge, US, 2010) [accessed June 16, 2011]. Extract from Paula Ramirez's field notes in which she reflects upon her meetings with Catarina, a resident of the City of Women.
3 In the spring of 2010, a Colombian researcher named Paula Ramírez traveled to Cartagena in order to interview the leaders of the Liga, including one of its founders and current director, Patricia Guerrero, and to visit the City of Women. (Ramirez Diazgranados, Patricia, 'Notas De Campo: Marzo 15 Al 19 Del 2010,' Field notes [accessed June 16, 2011].

Conclusion
Human rights education and peacebuilding—promises, challenges, and outcomes

The promise

In post-conflict contexts human rights education does in fact make good sense. The evidence for this is apparent in all of our cases: local educators have deemed education about human rights to be central to peacebuilding. They chose human rights education because they were aware that it would bring immediate, desirable, and necessary changes to the people they were working with in places where resources are scarce. All the educators in this study held firm to the belief that an educated population, particularly one educated in human rights, can not only better meet its needs, but also over time, influence national trends and processes to its benefit. In this conclusion we seek to identify those elements and forms of education that the educators, and we the authors, found to be most beneficial to long-term political and economic change and peaceful relations in the societies in question. All of this amounts to the real promise of human rights education in peacebuilding situations.

While the need for such education is generally acute, it is especially vital when it comes to the lives of women and children. In many nations, we have seen the emergence of the realization that women (and less so) children have equal rights to those of men. But these are not civil rights movements. These are human rights movements because they are grounded in universal human rights articulated in various international treaties and declarations connected to international institutions. In more ways than we the authors anticipated at the beginning of our work, almost all the educators settled on women and young people as their main educational targets for human rights education. Women, and increasingly young people, are the most active promoters of human rights of their own and those of other people.

Women and children have suffered the most from the high level of violence and abuse during, and even after conflicts. After conflicts, community and family tensions are complex, and domestic violence is rampant. For various reasons women and children, who have not been historically part of the reconstruction, are in reality responsible for family survival. On a policy and intergovernmental level, during the early 2000s, the rise of women's issues and women's rights was evident on the agendas of every national government. Perhaps it was simply lip service at first, but these government pronouncements about women and children have opened the door to the real changes that are seen in these chapters.

The educators also found that women are open to the idea that they become agents of their society's betterment, as well as of their own. The educators' needs assessment of women as the preferred target groups proved correct in all our studies, in the sense that they were the most immediately responsive. It was primarily, but not exclusively the women who responded to the message of the educators. In the women's eyes, they and their children had been the victims of male-generated violence, both systemic and domestic. Thus, having been forced to become agents of change by the need to survive during and after the conflict, women were not willing to return to the past and thus were ready to embrace the new human rights norms offered by the educators. Human rights education became a way to replace the more oppressive rules and customs that they had once accepted in their former, traditional patterns of living.

Further, in all our cases we found evidence that when people see the benefits of human rights education, they demand more of themselves and of the organizations that promote them. The educators found strong local demand for the education and skills they offered because the communities where they worked saw that this education would improve their daily lives. The felt-needs voiced by the communities were very much in line with what the human rights educators promised or could respond and adapt to. Traumatized by years of rape, murder, and other forms of violence, as well as by the loss of relatives and property, the survivors wanted to know how to prevent such miseries in the future. The demand for the needed education and skills was especially acute in the early period as the violence subsided. This was visibly the case in the Liberia and Colombia studies. When the education programs began, the armed actors were still active in the region and enjoying impunity. The national governments were still unable to assure human security in all communities across the whole country. In these cases the human rights educators were able to meet local demand by showing the communities how human rights provided rules and processes which, when combined with analytical and conflict-management skills, enabled the communities to becomes actors able to resolve some, if not all, of their problems.

All the educators promote the idea that children have rights, but this idea does not receive recognition in the cultural practices and norms in the societies where they were working. The struggle for equal recognition is even more difficult for children, and their participation in decision-making. As a result of their lack of recognition in many parts of the world, very young children were used as income-generators working the streets as best they could to find survival income for their families or other support system. This values-conflict situation was faced by the program in Chiapas, Mexico, as well as by the secondary school program in Senegal. The latter was especially effective in generating sympathy for the students on the part of the teachers, and empathy among the students for people suffering rights abuses in the surrounding communities, especially street children.

We were interested in how human rights education inspires and empowers youth, and how it directly applies to their lives. The study on secondary school education in Senegal, for example, takes credit for using art and other forms of expression to enhance empathy on the part of students for other people, especially other children, suffering human rights abuses. The Senegal human rights education program turned the students' school into a safe space where emotional needs are prioritized, where the students are encouraged to engage in dialogue about subjects that matter a great deal to them, and where they can build and strengthen ties with their fellow classmates. As a whole the cases convey this information in ways that are both exploratory and descriptive.

The projects we studied, however, do not address the larger problem of the millions of young men and women who, with little or no education, are entering adulthood with few marketable skills to support themselves, let alone a family. This situation is especially serious in countries like Liberia which, although reasonably endowed with natural resources, lacks the communications and development systems necessary to employ a significant segment of its youth. If the goal of human rights education in countries emerging from civil war is "never again," a future with large numbers of unemployed and potentially disruptive youth should be a major concern for the government. While we want to teach the new generation about human rights for the future benefit of the world, children also need solutions for the present.

In the remaining parts of this conclusion we will explore three additional findings that address these questions: (1) how does human rights education address violence by preventing violations and improving structural conditions, thereby contributing to broader peacebuilding goals? (2) What are the linkages between culture and HRE in peacebuilding contexts? And (3) how can HRE be both sustainable and self-propagating?

Findings on the impact of human rights education

The studies in this book are used as a vehicle to increase our knowledge of how human rights educators foster social change and forge linkages with broader peacebuilding goals. The major educational goal of all the programs was certainly that of enhancing human security, and in particular the elimination of domestic and systemic violence against women, especially by encouraging the women to become agents rather than seeing themselves as just victims. This transition is vividly illustrated in the story of the teacher in Sierra Leone who discovered that one of her ten-year-old students was being raped regularly by her uncle. In the study, the teacher describes how she was able to overcome the threats of the man, the lack of response by the police, and the fears of the child in order to bring the man to court and effect a conviction. Critical in the teacher's change of consciousness was the realization that family rape was not a private matter but a public crime. The other major educational goal in all the programs was to convince the target populations, notably the women and adolescents, that they have rights, such as those to education and freedom from sexual exploitation. Education which gave access to legal redress in cases of violence against women were the primary goals of the projects in Cusco, Peru, and in Cartagena, Colombia.

Human rights education can achieve social impact in many ways. In our studies we found that it helped communities to help settle property and other disputes that had arisen during conflict, and to develop within the community the institutions needed to maintain peace and security as well as to promote economic and political development. Human rights education programs helped people to organize and address their immediate problems as a community. This dimension was especially appreciated on the part of villagers in the Liberian study. They recognized and welcomed the economic benefits of speedy and effective conflict resolution based on the institutionalization of human rights principles and practices in the work of their local Community Peace Committees. The education was found to empower individuals through the acquisition of the knowledge that rights have a legal basis and can be enforced in the courts. It enables citizens to know that they and others have rights, and thus with the knowledge that they can be brought to justice, to dissuade those who seek to abuse those rights. Human rights education also provides a community with a common and unifying set of goals, mobilizing the community to remedy an abuse that affects them all. Claiming their rights in the courts by the community as a whole has been at the heart of the human security strategies of the City of Women in Colombia. The women learned the value of documenting rights violations and bringing them to the attention of the local authorities and the international community. These are all important HRE-based outcomes that enable post-conflict communities to rebuild.

To assure the sustainability of their work, the various educators looked to capacity-building for their local activists. Typically this took the form of short training workshops. In Sierra Leone, for example, the national section of Amnesty International held such workshops to enable local educators, notably teachers from public schools in different parts of the country to meet and share skills and experiences. The interactive, problem-solving style of the workshops set the pattern for the participants' later work in the field. There and elsewhere the local educators were trained to make extensive use of theatre and music in the local communities and to stimulate public debate after the drama or other activities. A common topic was the choices and dilemmas associated with the social status of women and their health needs. The expectation was that techniques used in the workshops would be replicated in trainees' home communities.

Human rights education, culture, and peacebuilding

The various analyses in this volume of how human rights education contributes to re-building communities after a conflict underline its primary role and thus its promise, namely to bring new norms, practices and institutions to the communities. These new modes are based on the international human rights laws and practices which now define the associated obligations on government and thus also on government officials. The primary normative reference point of the educators we studied was the modern international human rights regime which is now recognized as a major and integral component of international law and international relations. That regime consists of treaties, practices and institutions that obligate the world's governments to a set of standards that govern the way they treat all persons living within their respective jurisdictions. Although many states have not ratified all the treaties, most states have ratified enough to have obligated themselves to a substantial segment of standards and thus to have subjected themselves to international supervision and enforcement. Enforcing the resulting obligations on states is the core promise of the human rights regime and thus a major goal of human rights education. The particular challenge in communities recovering from violent conflict is what happens when the presence of government and government institutions is weak and ineffective.

On account of its powerful role in conditioning human thinking and behavior, culture—as the complex of established values, behaviors, and relationships within a given community—presents both a challenge and a resource for human rights educators. The project with children in Mexico, for example, highlights the need to relate human rights education to both the daily experience of the children, and to the impact of the local cultural heritage on life as a child. For the educators, culture was an obstacle because the traditional culture did not recognize children as having rights. It was a challenge to teach the idea of children as subjects of rights and freedoms, especially with respect as to how their rights and freedoms evolve as they grow older. The rights and freedoms that a one-day-old child might claim are quite different from those of a child on the verge of adulthood. Thus the full target group stretched from their parents to the society at large and especially to government officials such as the local police officers who have to deal with children when they encounter them working on the streets. On the other hand, as the children were already deeply versed in that culture, its stories and worldviews, the educators could draw on those images and thought patterns to convey, if not also to justify, their new ideas.

In the case of Sierra Leone the educators realized even in their original needs assessment that they were taking on not just the consequences of the war, but also deep cultural and religious traditions that for centuries had endorsed serious inequalities between the sexes including the toleration of domestic violence. The patterns of gender discrimination and other abuses in traditional society had largely been invisible or seen as insignificant and natural. They were thus culturally endorsed. Moreover, as that study outlines, women's low social status was also closely related to the state of systemic poverty associated with being a woman in traditional Sierra Leone. It took the civil war for the women to realize how they had been cowed into silence by many social forces including their own shame, fear of reprisal, fear of losing their bread-winner, and fear of being stigmatized in their own communities. A new consciousness along similar lines was visible in all the communities we studied, most notably in the Cusco study. The challenge faced by the educators was to find ways in which human rights and human rights education could be used to bring redress.

The overall challenge that surfaced in virtually all the cases was to address the violence and other tensions within the communities that were either pre-existing, or had arisen on account of the conflict, so that both would be less likely to arise in the future, in other words meeting the goal of "never again." This basic tension resulted in a second challenge, namely the tension between traditional practices, notably gender relations, and the content and methods of the human rights educators. This is not to say that traditional practices were a major cause of the conflict, only that some of them aggravated it. In some international circles these issues raised ethical concerns, in the sense that the communities and cultures in which the educators were working were at the time weak and disorganized, and the educators came from outside the community, with access to resources which the community did not possess and yet needed. However, these ethical concerns were not raised by either the researchers or their interlocutors in the field research. Rather, as indicated above, the human rights education programs were designed and evaluated by the educators in terms of their respective beneficial impact, namely how human rights principles and norms could enable the communities in question to create the practices and institutions needed to help them rebuild and hopefully also to reduce the likelihood of a future conflict. The core of the external input was the norms, together with the knowledge and skills needed to implement those norms.

What have we learned about outreach and sustainability?

Another major consideration for the educators and planners of human rights education is sustainability, that is the ability of projects to survive and grow through a multiplier effect after the external inputs (personnel, financing and technology), and agents have withdrawn. At a basic level, the common major challenge facing all the projects was access to finance. Virtually all the funding as well as expertise for the projects came from outside the communities themselves. The scope, format and duration of each project studied were governed entirely by the amount of funds obtained from outside the community. Even the City of Women in Colombia still relies on continued external funding. Under-financing is common to development projects in all rural areas, which are at the end of the supply chain. They are at the end of the supply line. In this study even the MA program at PUCP in Lima, with its broad goals of nation-wide reform, was underfunded. Most students had to pay the same fees as students in other programs leading to more lucrative careers in law and business. Continuing access to funds is crucial to assure the sustainability and growth of any new program.

The multiplier effect is no less challenging. The obvious achievements in this respect were the teachers in Senegal who changed their teaching methods quite radically and planned to teach that way for the foreseeable future, as well as the City of Women, in which the women built permanent houses and lived together in them as a community where human rights were cherished as respected norms. Moreover, in Senegal, other teachers in the school were voluntarily adopting the human rights-based methodologies. However, the graduates of the Malick Fall school in Senegal and the MA program in Peru found it difficult to find remunerative employment that used their human rights knowledge and skills, let alone employment that built these same capacities in others. One multiplier effect that was largely unmet in practice among this group of studies was that of integrating the human rights education into larger educational and other systems. Except the university program in Lima and the Malick Fall secondary school in Senegal, the human rights education programs were stand-alone activities enjoying only moral and financial support from government officials or international agencies and programs. To be sustainable HRE needs to be a formal, funded component in international peacebuilding and development mandates and in national educational planning as a whole.

The City of Women study provides another insight into how human rights education is reinforced significantly and becomes more sustainable when it becomes part of the daily life and conversations of the community as a whole. To quote the text: "Learning does not reside within individual persons, but rather within the various conversations of which they are a part." In this case two tangible forms of sustainability were apparent, namely, the physical presence of the now more than one hundred permanent houses and related community services, and, secondly, the life-long skills in management and democratic life acquired by the women.

In Sierra Leone, sustainability and growth were sought by encouraging local communities to form their own human rights clubs and to organize their own dramas and discussions once the external agents have moved on. The goal was one of consciousness-raising, which gained impetus because of the questioning of traditional norms resulting from the excesses committed during the conflict. In Senegal sustainability and growth relied on providing the teachers with substantial training in human rights teaching. They were taught to use a wide range of methodologies to help students identify, analyze, and seek to bring redress to a problem that affected their community and which is being changed through public policy or community action. The students were taught to integrate reports and debates about the ongoing conflict, and to encourage the students to analyze real-life problems in their community. Part of that analysis called for them to take into consideration any relevant laws and policies that the government might have adopted that affected the problem. Using this analysis and the underlying research, the students then generated a plan to address the problem and implement it outside the classroom.

The MA program at the university in Lima, Peru, also made outreach its challenge. Its aim was to design a model that would attract young professionals and enable them to integrate human rights into their respective professions and careers, as well as into their lives as citizens committed to a democratic future for Peru. This group, especially the future lawyers and teachers among them, were seen to be essential multiplier agents. As in the case of the program in Senegal secondary school, a multiplier effect was generated by the teachers who took on the task of teaching the new human rights courses, finding the preparation of the courses, the teaching experience itself, and the associated interaction with the other faculty members teaching in the program, to be personally beneficial and enriching in themselves. Given the size of the population of countries like Peru that face continuing serious human rights abuses both with and without a civil conflict, it will take larger and more advanced programs than the scale achieved in Peru.

Implicit in much of this study is the awareness that the governmental and non-governmental institutions in existence in those societies prior to the conflict were ill-equipped to prevent the conflict. Missing completely in these studies and very limited in practice elsewhere, are human rights education programs that focus on the very government officials that are legally bound to protect all the human rights of their fellow citizens. Moreover, although we did not seek to identify all the other human rights education programs in the countries we studied, it is clear that human rights education activities tend to be self-contained activities and not an integrated component either of larger peacebuilding activities or partnerships, or of the national curricula. The conclusion from these findings is that if the educational institutions of a country are to equip large numbers of teachers with the knowledge, skills and attitudes which the studies in this volume have shown to be necessary for peacebuilding, the public and private institutions must expand their activities substantially.

To be truly sustainable, human rights education needs to be institutionalized, such as by becoming part of the approved curricula in the public school system and being taught by appropriately trained teachers. The Senegal study shows how appropriate training results, not just in good choices with respect to the material taught, but also in the way it is taught. In our studies, the Senegal case exemplified the radical nature of the change in attitude on the part of the teachers towards their students that was highly appreciated by both parties. This outcome is further evidence of the need to develop human rights curricula that promotes learning in skills, behavior and attitudes, in addition to increased knowledge of human rights law, principles and institutions. Evidence of sustainable beneficial outcomes was also recorded with respect to impact on third parties, such as school teachers in Chiapas, Mexico, and the government officials in Cusco, Peru.

Human rights education and peacebuilding: challenges and opportunities

The answer to the question "how" does human rights education reduce violence and build peace is conditioned by the choice of target group, course content and the methods used in each human rights education program. The studies confirmed the choice of the common core concepts associated elsewhere with human rights education, namely: (a) that the content is defined by the international human rights documents; (b) that it overlaps with education in other fields, notably transitional justice, citizenship, rule of law, conflict management and economic and political development; (c) that its goals focus on promoting the economic and political emancipation and empowerment of both individuals and their community; and (d) that the adoption of human rights norms require adjustments to long-standing social and cultural practices.

As far as teaching methods are concerned, there was a fairly broad consensus on the importance of participatory rather than didactic methods of learning, as well as on content and methods that prepare learners directly for their daily life and for advocacy outside the classroom. This study focused on how these general goals and methods played out in the context of different target populations (notably rural women, youth, children, and young professionals) in the seven societies emerging from violent civil conflict. In a nutshell the promise of the human rights education was that it would make a difference in people's daily lives, that theory makes a difference in practice.

Second human rights content was seen to call for, and even impose, a certain basic type of teaching, namely one that encouraged the implementation in real life of the knowledge, norms, skills, attitudes, and behavior that are associated with a human rights framework. Central to that process in the eyes of most of the human rights educators is empowerment, namely enabling individuals and communities to move from seeing themselves as victims to become agents for positive social change. In addition to empowerment which is based on the knowledge of having rights, the human rights educators in different ways focused on the development of three other skills in particular, namely critical thinking, joint problem solving, and conflict management. To respond to the effects of the different conflicts, most of the programs encouraged the learners to see themselves as actors seeking social change and improvements in their communities.

Virtually all the studies found that if human rights education is to reduce violence in the long run, HRE should not be a stand-alone activity. It needs to be buttressed by additional skills (such as joint-problem-solving conflict management and dispute resolution), by an economy that enables the citizenry to earn enough to support themselves and their families and to live in dignity, and by institutions that provide sustained education and "solve inevitable social conflicts before any of the parties feel the need to turn to violence." Within this larger picture, one role unique to the various human rights education programs is that they create a space within which ordinary, even illiterate, citizens are exposed to human rights and encouraged to think critically about their situation, and about how they can improve it. This reflects an understanding of human rights education as more than just having rights, but also knowledge of those rights and organization in order to attain them. The paradigm shifts implied in this saying (new knowledge, agency, empowerment, mobilization, and institutionalization) are common, if not core, to most human rights education programs in ways that are not necessarily true in the practice of other approaches to political and economic development, and development aid.

These conclusions respond to the words of the Preamble to the UN Charter, namely that human rights abuses are a cause of war and conflict. Eliminating those abuses calls for a society-wide culture and practice of human rights and social justice in order to ensure a reasonable degree of peace and economic well-being. This is the belief and the goal that underpins the work of human rights educators. The cases in this book reflect on this promise, but a more precise assessment of how HRE, and which forms of HRE can reduce violence requires monitoring over a longer period and across a greater range of programs to show how human rights education does make a significant and systemic difference.

Bibliography

Abdi, A. and Lynette Shultz (2008). "Six: De-subjecting subject populations, historico-actual problems and educational possibilities." In *Educating for human rights and global citizenship* (pp. 65–80). Albany, NY: State University of New York..

Abdullah, Hussaina J. and Aisha Fofana-Ibrahim (2010). "The meaning and practice of women's empowerment in post-conflict Sierra Leone." *Development, 53*(2),: 259–266. June 2010

'African Human Rights Education Project' (2010). Amnesty International [database online], accessed 22 June 2011. www.amnesty.org/en/human-rights-education/projects-initiatives/ahrep.

Akinsulure-Smith, Adyinka M., Lynn L. Amowitz, Kristina Hare Lyons, Binta Mansaray, Chen Reis, Louise Taylor, Beth Vann, and Vincent Iacopino (January 23/30, 2002). "Prevalence of war-related sexual violence and other human rights abuses among internally displaced persons in Sierra Leone." *JAMA: The Journal of the American Medical Association, 287*(4): 513–521.

"An agenda for peace: Preventive diplomacy, peacemaking and peace-keeping" (1992). New York: United Nations, A/47/277 – S/24111. www.un.org/Docs/SG/agpeace.html.

Archibald, Steven and Paul Richards (2002). "Converts to human rights? Popular debate about war and justice in Rural Central Sierra Leone." *Africa: Journal of the International African Institute, 72*(3): 339–367.

Ariza Altahona, Alexis, Lina Gonzalez Pineros, and Patricia Guerrero Acevedo (2009). "Desde el corazon de las mujeres: Una estrategia de resistencia juridica de la liga de mujeres desplazadas," Cartagena de Indias: Liga de Mujeres Desplazadas. www.observatoriogenero.org/DDV/desde%20el%20corazon%20de%20las%20mujeres.pdf.

Auerback, Carl and Silverstein, Louise (2003). *Qualitative Data: An Introduction to Coding and Analysis (Qualitative Studies in Psychology)*. New York: NYU Press.

Bajaj, Monisha (March 2004). "Human rights education and student self-conception in the Dominican Republic." *Journal of Peace Education, 1*(1).

Bajaj, Monisha (2011). "Human rights education: Ideology, location, and approaches." *Human Rights Quarterly, 33*(2): 481–508.

Bandura, Albert (1986). *Social foundations of thought and action*. Englewood Cliffs, NY: Prentice Hall.

Bandura, Albert (1997). *Self-efficacy: The exercise of control*. New York: W.H. Freeman.

Barnett, Michael, Hunjoon Kim, Madalene O'Donnell, and Laura Sitea (2007). "Peace building: What is in a name?" *Global Governance, 13*(1): 35–58.

Baxi, Upendra (1994). *Human rights education: The promise of the third millennium*. New York: United Nations, Organizing Committee of the People's Decade of Human

Rights Education [accessed 20 June 2011], www.pdhre.org/dialogue/third_millenium.html.
Bellows, John (2006). "War and institutions: 'New evidence from Sierra Leone'. *American Economic Review*, *96*(2): 394–399.
Bellows, John and Edward Miguel (2009). "War and local collective action in Sierra Leone." *Journal of Public Economics*, *93*(11–12) (12): 1144–1157.
Benoit, Christine, n.d. *El proceso de cambio en las y los defensores comunitarios de la región Cusco*, Lima: Instituto de Defensa Legal, consultado el 31 de enero de 2011. www.justiciaviva.org.pe/genero_justicia/documentos/proceso_cambio.pdf.
Benoit, Christine, n.d. "Investigación sobre los beneficios de los servicios de las Defensorías Comunitarias en la región Cusco," Lima: Instituto de Defensa Legal, consultado el 31 de enero de 2011. www.justiciaviva.org.pe/genero_justicia/documentos/informe_beneficios.pdf.
Benoit, C. and V. Badajoz (2010). La educación en derechos humanos y la habilitación de capacidades locales para mejorar el acceso a la justicia de las mujeres indígenas afectadas por la violencia: el caso de las Defensorías Comunitarias del Cusco (unpublished).
Bernath, T., T. Holland, and P. Martin (1999). "How can human rights education contribute to international peace-building." *Current Issues in Comparative Education (CICE),* Teachers College, Columbia University, NY, *2*(1).
Betancourt, Theresa S., Jessica Agnew-Blais, Stephen E. Gilman, David R. Williams, and B. Heidi Ellis (2010). "Past horrors, present struggles: The role of stigma in the association between war experiences and psychosocial adjustment among former child soldiers in Sierra Leone." *Social Science & Medicine*, *70*(1): 17–26.
Bigmore, Pablo and Raúl Pérezgrovas Garza (2003). "Vida cotidiana en las colonias indígenas en la zona peri-urbana de San Cristóbal de Las Casas," en *Anuario de Estudios Indígenas* IX, Chiapas, Instituto de Estudios Indígenas de la Universidad Autónoma de Chiapas, pp. 13–61.
Brandt, Hans-Jurgen and Rocío Franco (comp.) (2010). *Las mujeres en la justicia comunitaria: víctimas, sujetos y actores*, Lima: Instituto de Defensa Legal, Serie Justicia Comunitaria en los Andes, Perú y Ecuador, Volumen 3.
"Brahimi Report," Report of the panel on United Nations Peace Operations [A/55/305] August 21, 2000.
Bronfenbrenner, Urie (1979). *The ecology of human development*. Cambridge, MA: Harvard University Press.
Bunch, Charlotte (1990). "Women's rights as human rights: Towards a re-vision of human rights." *Human Rights Quarterly*, *12*(4) pp. 486–498.
Bureau of African Affairs, 'Background Note: Liberia 2011. www.state.gov/r/pa/ei/bgn/6618.htm [accessed June 13, 2011].
Burton, John W. (1990). *Conflict: Resolution and prevention*. London: Macmillan.
Celis, Barbara (2010). Entrevista con Ann Veneman, Directora del Fondo de Naciones Unidas para la Infancia (UNICEF). Lo difícil es hacer cumplir la ley, *Defensor*, México, Comisión de Derechos Humanos del Distrito Federal, pp. 15–18.
Centro de Derechos Humanos Fray Bartolomé de las Casas (2002). "Caminando hacia el amanecer. Informe especial sobre desplazados de guerra en Chiapas," Chiapas, Centro de Derechos Humanos Fray Bartolomé de las Casas, Chiapas, México.
Centro de Derechos Humanos Fray Bartolomé de las Casas (2005). "Carpeta Básica para talleres de Derechos humanos," Centro de Derechos Humanos Fray Bartolomé, Chiapas, México.

Cepeda-Espinosa, Manuel Jose (2006). "How far may Colombia's constitutional court go to protect IDP rights?" *Forced Migration Review* (Special Issue: Putting IDPs on the Map: Achievements and Challenges (In Commemoration of the work of Roberta Cohen) (December 2006): 21–23 [accessed June 6, 2011].

"Child Right Act" (2007). *Sierra Leone Gazette Extraordinary*, CXXXVIII (43) 3 September 2007 [accessed June 14, 2011]. www.sierra-leone.org/Laws/2007–7p.pdf.

CODECC 2005, *Hablan las defensoras comunitarias: Una justicia distinta para las mujeres*, Lima: Instituto de Defensa Legal, pp. 30–122.

"Colombia: Displaced and discarded, the plight of internally displaced persons in Bogota and Cartagena" (2005). *Human Rights Watch*, *17*(4B), [accessed June 6, 2011].

"Colombian Constitutional Court, Decision no. T-025 of 2004" [accessed June 6, 2011]. www.brookings.edu/~/media/Projects/idp/Colombia_T%20025_2004.PDF.

Comisión de Derechos Humanos del Distrito Federal (2010). "Las niñas mexicanas: una población altamente discriminada," en Revista *Defensor*, México, Comisión de Derechos Humanos del Distrito Federal, pp. 61–64.

Comisión de Entrega de la CVR (2008). *Hatun Willakuy*, Lima, p. 9.

"Constitution of the Republic of Liberia" (1986). Liberia: National Legislative Bodies, [accessed 13 June 2011]. www.unhcr.org/refworld/docid/3ae6b6030.html

"Convención sobre los Derechos del Niño" (2009). México, Red por los Derechos de la Infancia en México.

"Convention on the Rights of the Child" (1990). United Nations Secretary General, 44/25. [accessed June 14, 2011]. www2.ohchr.org/english/law/crc.html.

Covell, K. and B. Howe (1999). "The impact of children's rights education: A Canadian study. *International Journal of Children's Rights*, 7: 171–183.

Dieye, Aminata (2010). L'impact du projet d'Action Citoyenne de CIVITAS/Sénégal sur la pratique enseignante et la vie des élèves dans la commune de Ziguinchor (unpublished).

Denov, M. and C. Gervais (2007). "Negotiating (in) security: Agency, resistance, and resourcefulness among girls formerly associated with Sierra Leone's revolutionary united front." *Journal of Women in Culture and Society*, *32*: 885.

Denov, Myriam and Richard Maclure (2001). "On their own and in their own words: Bolivian adolescent girls' empowerment through non-governmental human rights education." New York: Palgrave Macmillan, *Journal of Youth Studies*, *14*(2): 197 [accessed June 10, 2011] www.informaworld.com/10.1080/13676261.2010.506528.

Diop, N. J., E. Badge, D. Ouoba, and M. Melching (April 2003). "How 23 villages participated in a human rights-based education programme and abandoned the practice of female genital cutting in Burkina Faso," *Population Council.*

Diop, N. J., M. Faye, A. Moreau, J. Cabral, H. Benga, F. Cissé, Babacar Mané, I. Baumgarten, and M. Melching (August 2004). The TOSTAN program evaluation of a community based education program in Senegal, *Population Council.*

Dodd, Rebecca, John Hillary, and Andrew Mawson (2000). "War brought us here: Protecting children displaced within their own countries." London: Save the Children.

"Draft report of the working group on the universal periodic review," n.d., Geneva, Switzerland: United Nations General Assembly, Human Rights Council, A/HRC/WG.6/9/L.9. 2010 [accessed 10 June 2011]. http://lib.ohchr.org/HRBodies/UPR/Documents/session9/US/A_HRC_WG.6_9_L.9_USA.pdf [accessed June 10, 2011].

Ezpeleta, M. and K. Ouerdane (2010). "Community-based human rights impact assessments: Practical lessons. Report from an international meeting." www.dd-rd.ca/site/_PDF/publications/COBHRA_Report_en.pdf.

Fernández Liria, Carlos (1992). "Enfermedad, familia y costumbre en el periférico de San Cristóbal de Las Casas," *ANUARIO 1992*, Instituto Chiapaneco de Cultura: 11–57.

Flowers, Nancy and David Shiman (1997). "Teacher education and the human rights vision." In *Human rights education for the twenty-first century* (pp. 161–175) G. Andreopoulos and R. P. Claude (Eds.), Philadelphia, PA: University of Pennsylvania Press.

Flowers, N. and J. Lord (2006). "Human rights education and grassroots peacebuilding." In *Human rights & conflict: Exploring the links between rights, law, and peacebuilding* (pp. 431–459) J.W. Helsing and J.A. Mertus (Eds.), Washington, DC: United States Institute of Peace..

Forman, L. (2011). "Making the case for human rights in global health education, research and policy." *Full*, 207.

Fraga, Cristina P. (2007). "Colombia: La ciudad de las mujeres, refugio contra la violencia," *CIMAC Noticias: Periodismo con Perspectiva de Genero* [accessed June 17, 2011]. www.cimacnoticias.com.mx/site/07080207-Colombia-La-Ciudad.26819.0.html.

Freire, Paulo (1970). *Pedagogy of the oppressed*. New York: Continuum.

Geremia, Valeria (2009). "Índice de medición de calidad de leyes en el marco normativo de ellos derechos de la infancia," Red por derechos de la infancia, México DF.

Gervais, Christine (2010). "From discovery to dissidence: Honduran women's conceptions and claims of human rights." *Journal of International Women's Studies*, *11*(4) (05/01): 19–36, http://find.galegroup.com/gtx/infomark.do?&contentSet=IAC-Documents&type=retrieve&tabID=T002&prodId=ITOF&docId=A247222961&source=gale&srcprod=ITOF&userGroupName=nysl_se_vassar&version=1.0.

Gervais, Christine (2011). "From education to equality? Bolivian adolescent males understanding of gender equality in the wake of sensitivity workshops." In *Children's rights and international development: Lessons and challenges from the field*. Kathryn Campbell, Myriam Denov, and Richard Maclure. (Eds.), New York: Palgrave Macmillan.

Gervais, Christine (2011). "On their own and in their own words: Bolivian adolescent girls' empowerment through non-governmental human rights education." *Journal of Youth Studies*, *14*(2): 197, www.informaworld.com/10.1080/13676261.2010.506528 [accessed June 10, 2011].

"Global Appeal 2010–2011: Colombia" (2010). UNHCR: United Nations High Commissioner for Refugees. www.unhcr.org/4b02ca0e9.html [accessed June 7, 2011].

Gossen, Gary H. (1983). "Una diáspora maya moderna: desplazamiento y persistencia cultural en San Juan Chamula, Chiapas," *MESOAMERICA* 5: 253–276.

Guerrero, Patricia (2005). "La Tradición, La Semilla, y La Construcción. Sistematización de tres experiencias de resistencia de organizaciones de mujeres frente al conflicto armado en Colombia," *UNIFEM, Mesa de Conflicto Armada* www.observatoriogenero.org/DDV/publicaciones/tradicion_semilla_construccion_2005.pdf.

Guerrina, Roberta and Marysia Zalewski (2007). "Forum introduction: Negotiating difference/negotiating rights: the challenges and opportunities of women's human rights." *Review of International Studies*, *33*(1): 5–10 (January 2007).

Güezmes, Ana, Nancy Palomino, and Miguel Ramos (2002). *Violencia Sexual y Física contra las Mujeres en el Perú. Estudio multicéntrico de la OMS sobre la violencia de pareja y la salud de las mujeres*, Lima: C.M.P. Flora Tristán, Universidad Peruana Cayetano Heredia, OMS.

"Guiding principles on internal displacement" (2001). New York, NY: United Nations OCHA, Doc.E/CN.4/1998/53/Add.2 [accessed June 16, 2011].

"Hablan las defensoras comunitarias: Una justicia distinta para las mujeres" (2005). Lima: Instituto de Defensa Legal, p. 113.

Hafner-Burton, Emilie M. and James Ron (2009). "Seeing double: Human rights impact through qualitative and quantitative eyes." *World Politics*, *61*(02): 360. http://dx.doi.org/10.1017/S0043887109000136.

Hope, Anne and Sally Timmel (2000). *Training for transformation: A handbook for community workers*. Bourton on Dunsmore, UK: Intermediate Technology Publications, Ltd.

"HREA: The global human rights education network" (2011). In HREA: Human Rights Education Associates [database online], http://hrea.org/ [accessed June 12, 2011].

"Human Rights Report: Senegal 2009" n.d., US Department of State (US DOS) [accessed March 11, 2010]. www.state.gov/j/drl/rls/hrrpt/2009/af/135973.htm.

"Human Rights Report: Liberia 2010" (2011). Bureau of Democracy, Human Rights, and Labor [accessed June 13, 2011]. www.state.gov/g/drl/rls/hrrpt/2010/af/154354.htm.

Hvostoff, Sophie (2009). "La comunidad abandonada. La invención de una nueva indianidad urbana en las zonas periféricas tzotziles y tzeltales de San Cristóbal de las Casas, Chiapas, México (1974–2001)," en Marco Antonio Estrada (edit.), *Chiapas después de la tormenta. Estudios sobre economía, sociedad y política*, México, El Colegio de México, pp. 169–219.

Informe Narrativo Final (2009). Segundo Programa Especializado sobre Derechos Humanos de las Mujeres, IDEHPUCP.

"Introduction to peacebuilding" (2009). In International Association for Humanitarian Policy and Conflict Research [database online] accessed June 9, 2011. www.peacebuildinginitiative.org/index.cfm?fuseaction=cmc_printall.print&pageId=1681&printview=true&printchild=1.

Jennings, Todd E. (1994). "Self-in-connection as a component of human rights advocacy and education." *Journal for Moral Education*, *23*(3): 285.

Keen, David (2005). *Conflict and Confusion in Sierra Leone*. Oxford: James Currey.

Keller, Allen S., Sin Kim Horn, Sam S. Sopheap, and Gabriel Otterman (1997). "A Cambodian Human Rights Education Program for Health Professionals." In *Human Rights Education for the Twenty-First Century* George Andreopoulos and Richard Claude (Eds.), Philadelphia, PA: Pennsylvania University Press.

Lave, Jean and Etienne Wenger (1991). *Situated learning: Legitimate peripheral participation (Learning in doing: social, cognitive and computational Perspectives)*. Cambridge, UK: Cambridge University Press.

Liberia: Truth and Reconciliation Commission of Liberia, *Final report* 2008. [accessed June 14, 2011]. http://trcofliberia.org/reports/final-report.

"Liberia at a glance" (2011). World Bank [accessed June 13, 2011]. http://devdata.worldbank.org/AAG/lbr_aag.pdf.

Liberia: Comprehensive peace agreement between the government of Liberia and the Liberians United for Reconciliation and Democracy (LURD) and the Movement for Democracy in Liberia (MODEL) (2003).

Liberia: National report submitted in accordance with paragraph 15(a) of the annex to human rights council resolution 5/1* 2010, Geneva, Switzerland: United Nations General Assembly, A/HRC/WG.6/9/LBR/1 [accessed June 13, 2011]. www.internal-dsplacement.org/8025708F004CE90B/(httpDocuments)/6BF4A5966951F449C12577C1003807F3/$file/UN+HRC,+National+report+submitted+in+accordance+with+paragraph+15a+of+the+annex+to+Human+Rights+Council+resolution+5-1,+23+August+2010.pdf.

"Liberia's truth and reconciliation commission inaugurated; SRSG doss announces $500,000 donation from UNDP" (2006). UN Mission in Liberia [accessed June 10, 2011]. http://reliefweb.int/node/200538.

Liga de mujeres desplazadas (2011). "Un espacio para las mujeres victimas del desplazamiento forzado en Colombia" [accessed June 16, 2011]. www.ligademujeresdesplazadas.org/magazine/default.asp.

Macklin, Audrey (2008). "Legal aspects of conflict-induced migration by women." *Reproductive Health Matters*, *16*(31) (05/01): *22*(11).

Marks, Stephen (1997). "Human rights education in UN peace building: from theory to practice. In *Human rights education in the twenty-first century* G. Andreopoulos and Richard Pierre Claude (Eds.).

Márquez, C., Jaime (1996). *Promoviendo sensibilidad*, Lima: Instituto de Defensa Legal.

Maclure, R. (2009). "Reconstruction versus transformation: Post-war education and the struggle for gender equity in Sierra Leone." *International Journal of Educational Development*.

McDermott, Richard, William M. Snyder, and Etienne Wenger (2002). *Cultivating communities of practice: A guide to managing knowledge*. Boston, US: Harvard Business Press.

Melel Xojobal (2009). "Infancia indígena y trabajo en San Cristóbal de Las Casas, México. Sus actores y sus voces," México, Melel.

Mihr, A. and Peter Schmitz (2007). "Human rights education (HRE) and transnational activism." *Human Rights Quarterly*, *29*(4), 973–993.

Monkman, K., R. Miles, and P. Easton (November 2007). "The transformatory potential of a village empowerment program: The Tostan replication in Mali." *Women's Studies International Forum*, *30*(6), 451–464.

Murphy, F. and B. Ruane (2003). "Amnesty International and human rights education." Routledge, *Child Care in Practice*, *9*(4) pp. 302–307.

Mujica, Rosa (2009). "Que nos enseñen bonito: El trabajo Derechos Humanos y Equidad de Género en escuelas rurales de Quispicanchi, Cusco" copyright Instituto Peruano de Educación en Derechos Humanos y la Paz (IPEDEHP) and Fe y Alegría 44 pub. Lima.

National plan of action for the prevention and management of gender based violence in Liberia 2006, Liberia: Gender Based Violence Interagency Taskforce, GBV-POA [accessed June 13, 2011]. http://s3.amazonaws.com/dna_futures/original/65/National_Gender-based_Violence_Plan_of_Action.pdf?1352415241.

Nečasová, Lucie and José Luis Escalona (2010). Victoria, Educación en Derechos Humanos en Chiapas, México Infancia trabajadora en la organización Melel Xojobal (unpublished).

"New displacement and challenges" n.d. Internal Displacement Monitoring Center, Norwegian Refugee Council. www.internal-displacement.org/8025708F004BE3B1/(httpInfoFiles)/9A0C63B752E940FCC125774600275651/$file/Senegal_Overview_June10.pdf.

Noonan, James (2010). Background Paper. Independent project at Harvard University, Cambridge, US (unpublished). *Nothing left to lose: The legacy of armed conflict and Liberia's children* (2004). Watchlist: On Children and Armed Conflict [accessed June 10, 2011]. www.watchlist.org/reports/pdf/liberia.report.pdf.

Okin, Susan Moller (1997). "Feminism, women's human rights, and cultural differences." *Hypatia*, *13*(2, Border Crossings: Multicultural and postcolonial feminist challenges to philosophy (Part 1)) (Spring): pp. 32–52.

Pajares, Frank (2005). "Self-efficacy beliefs of adolescents". In *Self-efficacy during childhood and adolescence: Implications for teachers and parents* (pp. 339–367) Tim Urdin and Frank Pajares (Eds.), Charlotte, NC: Information Age Publishing.

Peruvian Truth and Reconciliation Commission (TRC), *Final report* 2001, Lima, Peru, [accessed June 14, 2011]. www.cverdad.org.pe/ingles/ifinal/conclusiones.php.

Peters, Krijn and Paul Richards (1998). "'Why we fight': Voices of youth combatants in Sierra Leone." *Africa: Journal of the International African Institute*, *68*(2): 183–210.
"Plan of action: World programme for human rights education" (2006). New York and Geneva: United Nations Educational, Scientific, and Cultural Organization; Office of the United Nations High Commissioner for Human Rights [accessed June 15, 2011]. http://unesdoc.unesco.org/images/0014/001478/147853e.pdf.
"Promotion and protection of the rights of children: Impact of armed conflict on children" (1996). United Nations Department for Policy Coordination and Sustainable Development, A/51/150 [accessed June 10, 2011].
Reconstruction and Development Committee (2009). Monrovia, Liberia [accessed June 13, 2011], www.liftliberia.gov.lr/content_list_sub.php?main=63&related=63.
Red por los Derechos de la Infancia (2009). "La infancia cuenta en México," Las niñas, México, Red por los Derechos de la Infancia.
"Report of the secretary-general on the implementation of the report of the panel on the united nations peace operations" (2000). Geneva, Switzerland: United Nations General Assembly, A/55/502 [accessed June 13, 2011]. www.un.org/peace/reports/peace_operations/.
"Report of the secretary-general on women, peace and security" (2002). Geneva, Switzerland: United Nations Security Council, S/2002/1154 [accessed June 16, 2011].
"Resolution 1325 (2000). Adopted by the security council at its 4213th meeting, on October 31, 2000" Geneva, Switzerland: United Nations Security Council, S/RES/1325 [accessed June 16, 2011]. www.un.org/events/res_1325e.pdf.
Rey de Marulanda, Nora and Francisco B. Tancredo (2010). "De la Innovación social a la política publica, Historias de éxito en América latina y el Caribe," CEPAL: Santiago de Chile.
Rice, Susan E. (2011). "Remarks by ambassador Susan E. Rice, US permanent representative to the United Nations, at an open security council debate on post-conflict peace-building and institution-building." New York: United Nations.
Robledo Hernández, Gabriela (2009). "Identidades femeninas en transformación: religión y género entre la población indígena urbana en el altiplano chiapaneco," México, Centro de Investigaciones y Estudios Superiores en Antropología Social (CIESAS).
Ruiz, Marta (August 30, 2008). "Fiesta de sangre," *Semana* [accessed June 16, 2011]. www.semana.com/nacion/fiesta-sangre/114966-3.aspx.
Rus, Jan (2009). "La nueva ciudad maya en el valle de Jovel: urbanización acelerada, juventud indígena y comunidad en San Cristóbal de las Casas," en Marco Antonio Estrada (edit.), *Chiapas después de la tormenta. Estudios sobre economía, sociedad y política*. México, El Colegio de México, pp. 169–219.
Rus, Jan (2009). "La lucha contra los caciques indígenas en los Altos de Chiapas," en *ANUARIO XIII* del Instituto de Estudios Indígenas de la Universidad Autónoma de Chiapas. Chiapas, IEI-UNACH.
Saidu, M. (2010). The African Human Rights Education Project in Sierra Leone (unpublished).
Salmón Gárate, Elizabeth (2010). Impacto de la educacion en derechos humanos: Maestría en derechos humanos Pontificia Universidad Católica del Perú (unpublished).
Sesay, Max Ahmadu (1996). "Politics and society in post-war Liberia." *Journal of Modern African Studies*, *34*(03): 395.
Smith, Alejandra (2007). "Los indígenas no hablan 'bien'. Defensores comunitarios, ciudadanía étnica y retos ante el racismo estructural en México." *Culturales*, vol. III, núm. 005, pp. 105–134.

Speed, S. (2004). *Rights in rebellion: Indigenous struggle and human rights in Chiapas.* Redwood City, CA: Stanford University Press.

Stellmacher, J. and G. Sommer (2008). "Human rights education: An evaluation of university seminars." *Social Psychology, 39*(1), 70–80.

Stranahan, S. Q. (2012). *Empowering women*, available at www.equitas.org/.

"Truth and Reconciliation Commission Act 2000" (1999). Sierra Leone: Truth and Reconciliation Commission (TRC) [accessed June 14, 2011]. http://web.archive.org/web/20051230045239/www.sierra-leone.org/trcact2000.html.

Tibbitts, Felisa (1999). "Prospects for civics education in transitional democracies: Results of an impact study in Romanian classrooms." Cambridge, MA: HREA: Human Rights Education Associates [accessed June 22, 2011]. http://hrea.org/erc/Library/research/RPaper_4–991.html.

Tibbitts, Felisa (2005). "Transformative learning and human rights education: Taking a closer look." *Intercultural Education, 16*(2): 107–113 [accessed June 16, 2011]. www.informaworld.com/10.1080/14675980500133465.

Thompson, L. (July 1, 2011). "The word on Women—Failure to protect: Enduring challenges for peacekeeping in the DRC," *TrustLaw.*

UNFPA (2012). *Empowering women through education*, available at www.unfpa.org/gender/empowerment2.htm.

United Nations Security Council October 31, 2001, *Resolution 1325* (2000).

United Nations General Assembly 1994, *United Nations Decade for Human Rights Education*, A/RES/49/184. 94th Plenary Meeting sess. December 23, 1994 [accessed June 14, 2011]. www.un.org/documents/ga/res/49/a49r184.html.

Universal Declaration of Human Rights 1948, Paris: United Nations, General Assembly, A/810 at 71.

US Agency for International Development (USAID) June 2006, "Evaluation of the USAID peace-building program in Casamance and sub-region." http://pdf.usaid.gov/pdf_docs/PDACI085.pdf.

Wenger, Etienne (1998). *Communities of practice: Learning, meaning, and identity.* Cambridge, UK: Cambridge University Press.

Wenger, Etienne, Richard McDermott, and William M. Snyder (2002). *Cultivating Communities of Practice.* Boston: Harvard Business Review Press.

Yarsiah, James (2010). Rights and Rice Foundation in Liberia (unpublished).

Index

Access to Justice Project 45
advocacy 29, 39, 46, 47, 50, 62, 68, 70, 79, 80, 81, 88, 89, 93, 96, 101, 111
African Human Rights Education Project 3, 6, 15, 16
Amnesty International 17, 18, 24
attitude: change in 43, 46, 47, 49, 49, 50, 58, 110

Betancourt *et al.* 15
Bunch, Charlotte 25

Cambodia 2, 10
Casamance xi, 3, 7, 8, 52, 53, 54, 56, 60, 61, 62, 63
child abuse 31
Child Rights Act 3, 16, 21
children: rights of 29
City of Women 95, 96, 97, 99, 100, 101
Community Defenders xiv, 7, 38, 39, 40, 41, 42, 43, 44, 45, 46, 47, 48, 49, 50
community development 48, 80, 83, 84, 88
Community Peace Committees (CPCs) 8, 81, 84, 85, 86, 87, 88, 89
conflict: management 84, 89, 104, 110, 111; prevention 4, 80, 81, 82; resolution 46, 80, 82, 85, 87, 89, 106, 111
Convention on the Rights of the Child (CRC) 3, 16, 54
critical thinking 15, 32, 59
culture: democratic 50, 66; indigenous 32; local 5, 39, 68; traditional 107
curriculum: human rights 81; interdisciplinary 68, 69, 70; traditional 56
Cusco xi, xiv, 6, 7, 8, 38, 39, 40, 41, 45, 46, 48, 49, 72, 106, 107, 110

democracy x, 54, 58, 66, 70, 72, 79, 83

DFID *see* UK Department for International Development
discrimination: ethnic xii, 66; gender xii, 3, 15, 28, 46, 96, 107
domestic violence 16, 19, 20, 28, 34, 36, 42, 43, 45, 47, 75, 92, 103, 104, 105, 107

education: formal 99; higher 20; informal 32; secondary 3, 35, 55, 77, 78, 104, 105
emancipation 111
empathy 59, 61, 100, 104, 105
employment 14, 15, 57, 69, 75, 93, 109
empowerment xii, 5, 11, 12, 28, 33, 36, 43, 45, 48, 74, 79, 84, 97, 98, 111
environment 5, 29, 32, 33, 38, 39, 43, 47, 57, 68, 69, 95

Freire, Paulo 32, 38, 72, 81
funding 3, 4, 10, 55, 69, 70, 74, 108

gender roles 49

health 20, 29, 31
healthcare 27
Human Rights Council 52, 78
Human Rights Watch 92

Institute for Legal Defense 38

justice: access to 15, 40

law: domestic x, xi, 4, 66, 81; international xi, 8, 16, 18, 24, 31, 63, 81, 94, 96, 106, 107; local 8, 49; national 17, 24, 85, 96
leadership 43, 44, 47, 48, 96, 97
League of Displaced Women xv, 8, 93, 94, 95, 96, 97, 98, 99, 100, 101, 102
Lerner Febres, Solomon 65, 67, 70, 72, 73

Maclure, Richard 15
Malick Fall School 3, 7, 54, 55, 56, 57, 58, 61, 62, 63, 109
maternal mortality 16, 17, 18, 19, 20, 21
Melel Xojobal xiii, xiv, 7, 8, 26, 27, 28, 29, 30, 31, 32, 33, 34, 35, 36, 37
methodology: educational 7, 75
military *see* armed forces
minorities 2, 28

needs assessment 7, 11, 17, 33, 65, 101, 104, 107

participation: child 24, 36, 37, 57, 58, 59, 59, 104; female 15, 24, 46, 85, 87, 94, 97, 100, 101; political 37
partnerships 4, 16, 17, 45, 50, 94, 110
peacebuilding x, xii, xiii, 1, 2, 3, 4, 7, 9, 10, 11, 12, 23, 68, 79, 80, 81, 82, 94, 103, 105, 106, 109, 110
pedagogy: human rights 81
police xii, 1, 16, 23, 27, 40, 41, 42, 52, 60, 72, 73, 74, 77, 78, 80, 105, 107
Pontifical Catholic University of Peru (PUCP) 7, 8, 65, 66, 67, 68, 72, 74, 108

Revolutionary United Front (RUF) 14
Rice and Rights Foundation xiv, 8, 79, 80, 81

self-reliance 81, 84

sustainability 9, 11, 24, 45, 51, 62, 102, 106, 108, 109; economic 102

target groups xi, 5, 6, 11, 39, 50, 68, 74, 87, 104, 105, 107, 110, 111; choice of 11, 110
Tibbitts, Felisa 10
traditional leaders xii, 14, 19, 23
training in human rights 4, 7, 20
transitional justice 1, 2, 110

UN *see* United Nations
UN Department of Peace Keeping Operations (DPKO) 2
UNESCO 3, 4
UNICEF 3, 4, 38, 39
United Nations 14
Universal Declaration of Human Rights (UDHR) 55, 81, 82
US Institute of Peace (USIP) xiii

violence: domestic 6, 9, 15, 16, 19, 20, 24, 28, 31, 34, 36, 40, 42, 43, 45, 47, 48, 49, 75, 92, 103, 104, 105, 107; political 17, 39

women: rights of 21
World Decade for Human Rights Education 3, 54

youth 14, 30, 32, 34, 61, 68, 86, 89, 105, 111

CPSIA information can be obtained
at www.ICGtesting.com
Printed in the USA
JSHW011320201219
3107JS00002B/5